Swimming the Channel

50

FARRAR
STRAUS
GIROUX

Swimming the Channel

SALLY FRIEDMAN

Farrar, Straus and Giroux
New York

LIBRARY OF CONGRESS CATALOGING-IN-PUBLICATION DATA
Friedman, Sally.
Swimming the channel / Sally Friedman.—1st ed.
p.   cm.
1. Friedman, Sally.   2. Swimmers—United States—Biography.
I. Title.
GV838.F75A3   1996   797.2'1'092—dc20   96-12311   CIP

for Paul

I turn wearily towards the lack of you,
hold still as if to hold you still.

—GABRIELLE GLANCY

Swimming the Channel

When we arrived that morning the lake was as still as death, shrouded in the slightest promise of fog. The water had the dark opacity of disaster, of depths not meant to be tested. Floating apprehensively through a hazy dream, I left Paul to take care of the basics, such as putting the canoe in the water. Silence prevailed, so that when the boat slid along the floor of the truck bed the noise jarred. I stepped out of my sandals, hitched my sweatpants above my ankles, and walked reluctantly down the boat launch, gasping as the water pierced my feet. It was as if it was solid and sharp, as if it were still the ice it had been but a few short weeks before. I stared into the pale mist ahead of me, glanced down the ramp toward the deeper water, turned around, and walked away. "Forget about it. Put the canoe back in the truck. I can't even get in that stuff above my ankles."

The water thermometer read 58°F., 40 degrees below my body temperature, 26 degrees above freezing.

Paul ignored me. I knew he was thinking that if I couldn't do this I wouldn't be able to make it across the Channel, and all my life, or at least for as long as I could remember, I had wanted to swim the English Channel. Because it was what I wanted, it had become what he wanted for me. Our neighbors, who had driven us here in their truck, were watching from a bench, warm and snug in flannel shirts, jackets, jeans, shoes, and socks. I had only taken off my flip-flops, barely wet my feet, and felt ready

3

to quit. They assured me they wouldn't think less of me if I changed my mind. Paul made no such assurance as he continued to load thermoses and towels into the canoe, using that reproachful silence to coax me into trying again.

I slowly, lingeringly made my way back down the boat launch. Somehow, this time, it didn't hurt as much. I should have known that would happen. It was a lesson learned again and again; one can get used to the cold gradually, slowly enough to deaden the pain. Once again I turned around, this time with determination in my step. I found my cap and goggles and pulled them on. That was the easy part. I took off my sweats in the 50-degree air and tossed them into the canoe, knowing that it would be a lifetime before I felt warm again. Shivering, covered with gooseflesh, my arms held tightly across my chest, I walked the ramp one last time. Paul sat floating in the canoe, tantalizingly out of reach. He encouraged me, praising my progress, cheering every inch, until I was in up to my neck with nowhere to go but toward him, and so I pushed off and started to swim. The shock was too great. An iron band instantly clamped itself around my forehead. I turned back, seeking the safety of solid ground, gasping for air as yet another tight band encircled my chest. Ten strokes and I was on dry land without making a dent in the nine miles ahead of me.

Experience had taught me that the water felt marginally warmer on the second try. Clinging to this memory, I steeled myself for another attempt. Paul was waiting and the neighbors were watching, and the quicker I started and the faster I swam, the sooner it would be over.

So I slipped back into that liquid ice and started swimming

for real. Paul was there instantly, my guardian angel gliding along at my side. The cold tightened my joints, making it difficult to lift leaden arms out of water that was surely heavier, darker than any I had ever encountered. I seemed clumsy, disjointed, not at all the way I usually felt while swimming. Tingling pinpricks turned my skin into something strange, a foreign substance separate from my body. "Numbness" is generally defined as the absence of feeling, but the process by which one achieves it is invariably painful. And when one arrives, it is clear that numbness is nothing more than agony in a different form.

Seeing the mud and weeds beneath me, I tried to convince myself that shallow water is always warmest, forgetting that the temperature difference is only noticeable at the end, when swimming into shore, into the warmth. It is then that the lake feels so comfortable that one wonders how it ever seemed cold. Instead of making my peace with the shallow water, I only increased my dread of the deep. I turned inside to my imagination for help, telling myself that I was an island of heat, pulling my way through a chill that couldn't touch me, but the ice cut straight through the lie. Even my teeth ached, as if I had bitten into ice cream. The sloshing of water in my ears, the rhythmic splashes of my arms and the oars were all I heard. In my head I tried to get a sound track going or a daydream or anything to keep my mind off the bitter frost. But even my mind was frozen; no thoughts lasted longer than an instant, the time it took for the cold to overcome any attempts to escape it.

We had agreed that Paul would stop me every hour for food —for this swim, mostly hot chocolate and chicken soup. When it seemed that an hour would never pass, I asked him to stop me every half hour, assuming that it had been at least that long since the start. Not only hadn't it been, but an eternity remained until that half-hour mark. When I finally paused, my hands shook uncontrollably as I gulped the hot liquid, feeling the warmth travel through my body as if tracing an anatomical road map. Treading water generated even less heat than swimming, so I didn't linger over those longed-for respites. At each stop, Paul reassured me: I was doing great, I looked wonderful, I was almost there; and I accepted what he told me, wanting desperately to believe what I, had I been rational, would have known could not be true.

At no time during that swim did I ever feel right, never swift and strong, never sure of reaching the end. While swimming usually brings out all that is graceful in me, that day I fought to free my arms from the water lest they be frozen in place. Each stroke shattered the brittle surface, every breath was a frantic gasp. I thought, Okay, I'll make it to the next half hour and then I'll get out. But then the hot chocolate would fool me with the illusion of warmth, and Paul would encourage me, and I'd think, Okay, that's better, maybe I'll go just a little farther. But then I couldn't stop until the next half hour was up, at which time the vicious cycle would repeat itself, until four hours and eighteen minutes later I walked out of the water, up the town beach, into the haven of Paul's waiting arms.

Intellectually, I knew that at some point in my life I would be warm again, but physically, it seemed an impossibility. My jaw was clenched, frozen into rigidity, so that when I attempted speech, I sounded like a drunkard. Two neighbors, Judy and her young daughter, Elizabeth, happened by, and were amazed at my feat, and at the odd shade of blue I was. Paul laughed and fussed and bundled me into the car, engine running and heat at full blast. The air lapped warmly at my skin, but it was out there beyond me, unable to penetrate my icy core. Paul finished tying the canoe to the top, loaded our gear, and climbed into the car, exclaiming at the heat, but I wouldn't let him turn it down. As we started to leave he said, "Where's that hand? I have to hold that hand." Searching through the towels and blankets, he found my trembling fists and pressed them tightly against his chest, slowly thawing me as he drove me home to the bliss of a steaming shower.

Toward the end of that swim, when I knew I would finish, it was only the dream of being enveloped in hot water, a sensation I could barely imagine, let alone remember, that kept me going. It is fascinating to me that one must stand under a hot shower, being pelted by heat for so long, for what seems like hours, to feel truly warm, through and through, whereas on a steaming-hot day, it takes no more than a few seconds in a cold shower to be refreshed, if not shivering. It must have something to do with the physical law that a body naturally cools, just as the sun is burning out, or the universe winding down. Warmth requires energy; in situations of extreme cold, one needs to stay in motion to avoid freezing to death.

In the midst of that Schroon Lake swim I was thinking that this experience had to put an end to my English Channel aspirations. I had always thought that I liked cold water, but this was surely beyond anything I could grow to like. And, like it or not, there was a reasonable chance that the English Channel in August would be as cold as Schroon Lake the first week in June, or as cold as Paradox Lake had been in May. Hypothermia is a very real problem in long-distance swimming. Several years ago a young woman, an experienced swimmer, died while attempting a Channel crossing. No one on her boat realized that the time had come to pull her out, and it was too late by the time they did. We were unsure whether we would know when or if that time had come for me. Paul worried more than I; somehow I was convinced that I would know when to stop and that it wouldn't be before I walked or crawled onto a French beach. I was willing to leave it to him to see to it that my body temperature did not drop irrevocably while at the same time giving me the chance to make it to the other side, no matter how much it hurt. In fact, Paul was so proud of me that after Schroon Lake I forgot how painful it had been and remembered only that I had done it. I have often thought marathon swimming must be like childbirth, or making a movie, in that one forgets the pain in time and the accomplishment becomes the dominant memory.

I have swum for almost as long as I have walked, at first because I had an aptitude, later because it soothed my soul, kept me sane. Swimming lessons began the summer I was three years old. Eighty percent of the newborn human body is water, and infants have a well-documented "swimming reflex." I doubt that the one has anything to do with the other, except that perhaps, on some metaphysical level, water and swimming are in our blood. Without cultivation, this instinct is lost before most people take advantage of it. I think I remember learning how to swim, but it is possible that my memories have become entangled in years of seeing others taught, slippery little children slithering through water, holding the hands of their teachers as they try to master the art of blowing bubbles, or turning their heads to the side to breathe. Those first few years, before I started competing, I swam only in the summer. Afraid that I would forget how to swim over the winter, I tried to practice in the bathtub.

My earliest trophy is dated 1960. I was four years old, almost five, and wore an inner tube because that was the rule. The race was half the length of the pool, from the rope across the middle to the wall at the shallow end. Each child was held by a parent, who pushed as hard as he or she could, to give their own the best start. I had already passed the deep-water test, as my mother has told friends and strangers so often that I almost remember it. I was allowed anywhere in the large pool, unsupervised. As the years passed, I felt more and more out of place at my parents' country club, but I still coveted that swimming trophy, there to be won at the end of every summer. I might not have been very popular but I could swim faster than anyone my age, boy or girl.

By the age of seven, I was swimming on a team. Workouts took place after school in the days before goggles. Most nights I lay on my bed with a cool, wet washcloth resting heavy on my face, soaking my burning, red-rimmed eyes. Maybe this is why I have always cried too easily, a tearing reflex meant to soothe the pain. Lights were nestled in multicolored halos, my bad eyesight blurry even with glasses. The advent of goggles sent swimming times plummeting. Athletes could suddenly train for thousands of yards without hurting their eyes. But they arrived too late for me. I had already given up. Most world-class athletes thrive on the adrenaline rush that races produce; the tension had the opposite effect on me. The starter's gun was fired and time stopped. I flew through the air, plunged into the water, arms outstretched, streamlined, and all that was familiar became strange. My rhythm was out of sync, the water slipped away from my reaching hands, my shoulders tightened like rubber bands ready to snap. I was one of the fastest swimmers on our local team but was put to shame whenever we had a national meet. The Olympics were never in my future. I retired from competitive swimming my senior year of high school, tired of losing to girls who had grown so much bigger and faster than I, tired of spending the better part of meets in the bathroom with a queasy stomach. But I never stopped swimming. I have the sense to know that it is what keeps me from going off the deep end.

JUNE 4, 1990

Paul returned to New York for the week; I stayed in Paradox to train in the cold water. I missed him, already having grown accustomed to seeing him every other time I breathed, even though we had barely started the outdoor part of the venture. Swimming miles in a pool without him was familiar; I had done it all spring, and most of my life. But from the first time I put a toe in that ice water that year he was there, teasing, being sympathetic, saying whatever needed to be said. In a sense, I was performing for him, showing him I could do what I said I would. The day after he left, the water felt a little icier, the effort it took to immerse myself seemed a little more difficult, but I knew I had to report back to him about how much I swam, and I knew I couldn't lie.

After waiting until midday, to eke out any available warmth from the sun, I had driven to the tiny beach at the far end of Paradox Lake. There was some serious chop and I was sprayed and splashed from what seemed like all directions, until I tried to return and realized that I was swimming into the wind. The waves slapped my forehead, pummeling me back. My hands and feet were already numb; all that existed beyond my ankles and wrists was stinging pain. I was not in the mood for the added degree of difficulty of a head wind; the cold was more than enough. I tucked my chin like a fighter ducking blows and forced my way through the churning water, cursing to myself, concentrating on keeping my strokes neat and efficient, in defiance of the chaos which engulfed me. The shore was too distant for me to know whether I was making progress, so I made myself assume that I was. There were no signposts, nothing to judge by, except my own confidence in my strength and swimming ability. Eventually I pulled near enough to the land to see the trees moving by, and then I knew that I was indeed nearing the end. My goals were so simple—a hot shower and a phone call to Paul—and so easily achieved.

My marathon-swimming career had been born seven years earlier, out of disappointment, out of a need to prove something. For the second time I had failed the United Scenic Artists exam (the test to get my union card), without which it was extremely difficult to make a living in my chosen field, painting scenery. For two years before this, I had worked on the Macy's Thanksgiving Day Parade, drawing floats mostly. When I was growing up, we spent the morning of Thanksgiving day in front of the television with cups of hot chocolate on TV trays. It gave me a secret thrill to be involved in something I had, as a child, admired from afar. The designer was a cheerfully exuberant man who often proclaimed, "Life is a paradox." Having seen it on a map, I teased him, saying, "Manfred, you know there's a town in upstate New York named Paradox." So one day, while visiting friends nearby, I drove north to visit this place and found, appropriately enough, that there wasn't actually a town, just a lake, and a post office. The name comes from the fact that at some times during the year the Schroon River serves as an outlet, at other times as a source. As I was exploring, trying to find a good swimming spot, I managed to get lost, although I didn't realize it for a while.

Driving down a dusty dirt road, peering through the trees, I spotted a house which stopped me in my tracks, and then I saw the for-sale sign—and the real-estate company had the very same name as mine. I pulled into the drive. It was midafternoon, the sunlight golden syrup. The sound of hundreds of grasshoppers formed a hushed kind of white noise. There was no car in front, no sign of life. I walked up the stairs to the front door, knocked, waited. When there was no response, I pushed open the massive wooden door and entered the silence of an empty house. I followed the light into a large room with vaulted ceilings, skylights, and enormous French windows, through which poured molten light. The house was bare of furniture, except for an eight-foot-long wooden plank table with a bench on either side. I had this fantasy of life lived as in a French or Italian movie, with good friends eating and talking at this table piled high with food and wine, a fresh breeze streaming through the open windows, children (someone else's, who would leave me in peace at the end of the day) laughing and running through the field.

I wrote down the phone number of the real-estate company. After swimming at the public beach on Paradox Lake, I drove through the town of Schroon Lake and spotted the realtor's office. Automatically, telling myself I was just asking, without thinking it through, I parked and walked in. A few months later I was renting the house, with an option to buy. I told myself the house was mine if I was accepted into the union the next year. Upon receiving notification to the contrary, I fled there, spending most of the weekend at the local YMCA, drowning my disappointment in the pool.

I returned to New York, at loose ends and lonely. A friend called and said she was thinking about swimming around Manhattan in the annual race, was I interested in joining her? What the hell, I thought. I may not be able to get into the union but I'll show them, I'll swim around Manhattan. I knew there was a flaw in the reasoning but I've never truly believed in logic, that every reaction is equal and opposite to the action which precipitated it, that a straight line is necessarily the best way to travel from point A to point B, that one's life will ever go as planned.

Marathon swimming was a new concept to me, one that seemed tailor-made to my personality. I loved the long training swims through open water. Morning and evening are the calmest times because the water and air temperature are synchronous. As the sun heats the air, wind currents are created which in turn push the water, causing waves. Rough water can be exhilarating and challenging, when it's not exhausting and annoying, but flat water will always be my ideal. The obsidian surface conceals the mossy liquid that falls away beneath me; the shafts of dusty sunlight frame my shadow deep below. Water-skiers seem to be late sleepers as a rule, and since they, too, like calm water, I cede the evenings to them. I join the silent fisherman in their faraway boats in the breathless still of dawn. Surely I am as fluid as I feel myself to be, barely skimming the surface of the silken lake, hardly leaving a wake to disturb the watercolor. My hand tilts just so, to slide into the water at an angle, choosing the path of least resistance. Then my arm glides forward, as far as I can reach before pulling back, feeling for maximum resistance in order to make progress, to move ahead. Every so often I try to concentrate on stroke mechanics, but mostly I prefer to lose myself in a daydream, or in the observation of the endless variations to be found by swimming the same route every morning, day after day. Because of all the differences in light, and temperature, and wind, and fog, and thoughts, repeating the same swim endlessly is rarely monotonous.

I read a story once about a man who went to an artist to commission a painting of a fish. Days passed, then months, then years. Finally the man was fed up, so he returned to the artist's studio to demand his painting. The artist took out his brush, dipped it in paint, and in minutes had painted a beautiful fish. The man exclaimed, "If it was that easy, why did I have to wait all these years?" The artist walked to a door, opened it, and out tumbled hundreds of paintings of fish. That is the essence of training, of rehearsing—doing something so many times that in the final instance it seems easy, effortless. Sprinters swim thousands of meters daily in order to swim their fastest fifty meters. I swam hundreds of miles so that a particular twenty-mile stretch would be attainable. One must enjoy the process as much as the result, the sense that one is at least heading in the direction of that perfect fish.

Over the years I tried to perfect my swimming, or at least improve it. There was one coach who told me I had a great natural stroke. It took me a while to understand what he meant. People would comment that I had a bounce or a wiggle or a way of lunging forward. I watched videotapes but didn't really see what they meant. Then another coach, who happened to be a friend, told me that I shouldn't worry about it, that I had an idiosyncratic, personal stroke, and that it wasn't slowing me down. It was mine, it was comfortable, it got me where I was going in a minimum of time.

Swimming technique has changed a great deal over the course of my life. Powerboats are faster than canoes, so it has been decided that the action and shape of propeller blades, instead of paddles, are to be emulated. Exercise physiologists have discovered that swimmers generate lift and thrust, much like that which allows an airplane to fly. The difference in the flow of water over and under a swimmer's hand and arm creates the same force as the air rushing above and below an airplane wing. An S-shaped path is the curve to follow, and the S is drawn three-dimensionally, by pulling out then in then out, at the same time as down then up then down. The slightest change in angle affects efficiency, and although the physiologists can observe and instruct, to a swimmer the best path is instinctual, the search for still water that will best propel one forward, and this is what the coach meant who complimented me on my "natural stroke." I know when my arm is moving ineffectually through the water, to save an aching shoulder, or out of laziness, and I feel the surge of strength that comes from catching the water just right.

As I teach Elizabeth how to swim, I notice that she is the only one at the crowded beach who actually puts her face in the water. The other children, untaught, lift their heads high and flail, trying to swim the crawl from what they have observed. They do not know that the most important part of swimming is that which they cannot see, for it happens underwater, and that although how one moves one's arms through the air matters, it is the least of it. The children, and most of the adults, struggle to keep their heads above water, not realizing how much easier it would be to put their faces down, to trust the water, and the pocket of air that will be there when they turn to the side to breathe. It seems so complicated when I try to teach all these things, from blowing bubbles to the S-stroke, but so simple when I do them, because I have done them so often. When I demonstrate something for Elizabeth, or just swim a little bit to loosen up, she exclaims that I make it look so easy. I try to slow the process down, to have her repeat each step until it comes naturally, and every year she improves, but because she swims only outside, winter interrupts us, so we start the following summer a bit behind where we finished the previous one.

There are two schools of marathon swimming. The first consists of those who want to swim from here to there, no matter how long it takes. The distance covered is all that counts. I watched someone swim trudgeon crawl for hours, an outdated stroke that combines the over-water recovery of crawl with a sidestroke kick. Frustrated, I couldn't understand why this man wouldn't take the time to learn to swim more efficiently, more quickly. The second school includes those who try to swim the distance in the least amount of time possible. That is what I aspired to, no doubt due to my past as a competitive swimmer, and my nature. A respectable time was as important to me as finishing. It annoys me that I'm not the fastest swimmer in the world, but I've grown accustomed to it. During Olympic years, I comb the early heat results to figure out what small, undeveloped country my times would qualify me to represent.

I swam around Manhattan twice the summer of 1983, then I bought the house, even though I didn't pass the test, even though I was only twenty-eight and on my own, barely scratching out a living. Often I make big decisions without thoroughly analyzing them, based mostly on intuition, on what I want to do instead of what I should do. Besides, I had learned how precious a haven can be when life doesn't quite work out. The week after the closing, I was off to France to stage-manage the European tour of a modern dance company. Coincidentally, it was in Paris several years before that I had dislocated my shoulder for the first time. As I was running down a flight of stairs, I stumbled. To save myself from falling, I grabbed the banister and in the process wrenched my shoulder out of its socket. The pain was excruciating but I didn't realize what had happened until I felt my arm grind back into place. The second time it occurred, in Mâcon, I recognized the pain. It took much longer that time to get my shoulder back together. A few days later in Mulhouse, I was giving a sound cue by holding my arm over my head, then dropping it at the appropriate time. My arm dropped right out of its socket as I fell to the floor, writhing in pain.

When I returned to the States, I called my doctor. He suggested I try physical therapy first, since the orthopedists were sure to recommend surgery. Three times a week for several months, I went for physical therapy. Then, while on vacation in the Caribbean, I was goofing around in the water, trying out some water-ballet moves. In fairly deep water, upside down, as if I were doing a handstand if the water were shallow, I was trying to see how high into the air I could raise my feet. With arms outstretched, I pushed against the water and forced my arm right out of its socket again. I came up for air, sputtering to the friend who was with me, "I've just dislocated my shoulder!"

My friend Mary, also a swimmer, offered to pull me in to shore. "No, that's okay. I can make it." I wasn't being a martyr; it was a question of pride, and self-sufficiency. Holding my right arm tight to my body with my left arm, I kicked my way to shore. The saltwater held me gently aloft and the real pain didn't start until I was on the beach.

In New York, I made the rounds of orthopedists. One told me I would be out of the water for up to a year, then was annoyed at the sight of a tear rolling down my face. The surgeon I chose told me that for baseball players he does such and such, for swimmers he prefers something else. That level of specialization appealed to me. I scheduled the operation for late spring, the day after the union exam. I was determined to try one more time, ignoring the fact that I was right-handed, and that it was my right arm which was a mess. My arm was slipping out of its socket with alarming frequency. Turning over in bed was all it took, and the pain was enough to make me nauseous and light-headed. By the time I received notice that I had failed the union exam yet again, I was more concerned with surviving with my right arm in a sling. The surgeon had found that my arm had become unattached from my shoulder and had replaced ligaments, which, like stretched-out rubberbands, cannot heal, with tendons, lacing everything back together.

I was back in the pool by summer, mostly just kicking and doing one-armed butterfly, which was easier than one-armed freestyle. By the fall, I was doing full workouts; the following summer I was racing long distances again. Ever since the operation, it has pained me to sleep on my right side, and I feel changes in the weather in my shoulder, so I worried that it would balk at all the training necessary for an attempt at the Channel. One afternoon, while working out at the health club, I was struck with searing pain when I lifted my right arm. I tried a few easy strokes, pulling my arm with as little pressure as possible through the water. I winced each time, turned around halfway to the other end, and swam breaststroke back, to avoid any overarm recovery. It was a Saturday in April; Paul was at the end of the lane. We still hadn't come to a definite decision about the English Channel. I worried that this could be the end, when I had barely started. We went home, where my shoulder felt fine, and I took Sunday off. Monday after work, it was with great trepidation that I pushed off the wall. I gently eased my arm out of the water, through the air, back into the water, and pulled myself forward. It was as if nothing had ever been wrong, no remnants of pain, no aches to remind me, and it was the last serious shoulder problem of the year.

The second Saturday in June found us once again up at dawn. We ate breakfast in the gossamer light, Paul and I together in a house afloat on cotton batting, waiting for the sun to melt the fog away from the windows. We had decided to do a round-trip journey of Schroon Lake, a swim I had done years before, but in 68-degree water. The distance would be comparable to the Channel—about twenty miles. Schroon Lake would be easier than the Channel in that I wouldn't have to face jellyfish or swells or the harshness of saltwater, but more difficult in that one is less buoyant in freshwater and therefore must kick more. There is no way to truly measure the distance of an open-water swim; between currents, wind, and simple wandering from a straight course, there are too many variables. Mileage covered does not necessarily equal distance swum. For instance, the circumference of Manhattan Island is usually given as twenty-eight and a half nautical miles. Because the swim is current-assisted, the actual distance swum is generally between fifteen and twenty miles.

We arrived at the town beach, on our own this time. There was no need for a second vehicle, as we were starting and finishing at the same point. During the summer there are floats and a roped-off swimming area. This early in the season, the beach seemed strange, primitive, without the normal signs of human activity, without the massive white Adirondack chairs lined sedately along the shore. The air was cool and damp, the sun nowhere to be seen, the mist saturated with the scent of balsam and wood smoke. I went about the process of forcing myself into the water while Paul methodically loaded the canoe. His calmness soothed me, his quiet reassured me. We were beyond words, as if in preparation for the swim, when I knew I would not be able to speak to him for long stretches. The communication was in having him at my side.

The wind picked up, churning the water into frothy whitecaps. The fog lifted, but only high enough to be absorbed into low-hanging, ominous clouds. It wasn't long into the swim before I realized that cold wasn't going to be the only problem. My right leg had hurt the previous weekend, but now the pain was such that I couldn't kick with it. This in itself was not an insurmountable problem, because in distance swimming the kick is insignificant. One need only kick enough to keep one's legs afloat; any more is wasted oxygen. The power and strength are purely upper-body.

Paul saw that I wasn't kicking and we stopped to discuss the problem about two hours into the swim. I held on to the boat while we talked, a forbidden act in the world of marathon swimming and the point of no return for that particular endeavor. Next thing we knew, I was in the boat to discuss the matter further. We had bought an unusually wide canoe at a garage sale, perfect for us because it was easy to climb into (too easy) and could be rowed by one person or paddled by two. I huddled in my towels, gulped down some hot chocolate, and we talked. Paul had taken on the mantle of coach with no experience and minimal understanding of swimming, but with a sense that there was little in life of which he was not capable. He didn't know whether to be tough or sympathetic, whether my injury was major or minor. The rule of thumb is that a dull ache is basic garden-variety pain and can be worked through, whereas a sharp pain signals potential injury. Most afflictions are somewhere in between, not so easily classified.

We drifted around the center of the lake, perplexed and unsure, but mostly procrastinating, until we saw a motorboat approaching us. As it neared, we saw that the driver was in uniform. I had a brief flash of humorous dismay, wondering if I would be arrested for getting out of the water, amazed at the guilt I felt for having been caught in the act.

The officer was skeptical when we explained that we had only one seat cushion because there was supposed to be only one person in the boat. As I understood New York State law on the subject, one flotation device was required per passenger. I would gladly have obeyed the law; I just hadn't planned on being a passenger. And really and truly, I could think of no hypothetical situation that could arise for which I would need a life preserver. Even though the water was frigid, even though my right leg was close to useless, we were never far enough from land that I wouldn't be able to reach it, even if I were carrying Paul. It is virtually impossible for a nonswimmer to understand how comfortable I am in water, how at home, how sure of myself. Maybe it was foolhardy, maybe it was naïve, but I truly felt invincible and could imagine nothing that would convince me otherwise.

One hot summer day we had gone for a swim in nearby Eagle Lake. There is an island in the middle of the lake on which a lodge once stood. The building had burned to the ground, leaving nothing but a stone chimney perched on the cliffs, overgrown after many years. It was only a few hundred yards from the shore, but there was no public access to that part of the lake, which meant that we had to climb over the guardrail to reach the water's edge. We had brought an inflatable raft so Paul could paddle to the island while I swam. Perched on the rocks near the lake, we started to blow it up only to find that the raft was riddled with holes, having spent many years in a closet, unused. Paul said he could swim that far, to the island, and that he really wanted to, that it wasn't worth scrambling back up the rocks to the car to drive to the store to buy a new raft. I told him I could always pull him if he grew too tired, but he was determined to do it himself.

As I swam slowly beside him, I had a sense of what all that water must feel like to one unaccustomed to it and slightly afraid of it. It made me nervous, and fearful, but only because I was seeing through Paul's eyes as he switched from crawl to backstroke to breaststroke. He was so proud of making it on his own, and so exhausted. While he rested, I swam off by myself, relieved to be moving freely, at my own speed, unencumbered. But knowing Paul was on the island made me anxious, as if I were missing something, so I didn't wander too far. When it came time to return, he willingly accepted the offer of a free ride. Floating on his back, he held on to my foot as I swam back. I felt that I could have swum forever like that.

We had a pleasant chat with the officer, promised to bring two flotation cushions next time, and received a stern warning. Thoroughly out of the mood, we turned around; still shivering, I forced myself back into the water and limped for home.

It was the first time I had ever quit in the middle of a swim, even a training swim. I thought it would be wonderful to be out of the water, to spend a free afternoon in lazy repose, but the shame outlasted the temporary pleasure. The sick feeling in the pit of my stomach was worse than any simple muscular pain. Paul assured me that he didn't love me any less for my failure, but I was convinced he was just being polite.

We theorized about cold water that weekend. I was increasingly frustrated by the fact that it wasn't any easier for me, that usually I was forced out the first time and cringed through the second attempt, that it still hurt so much. I was tired of numb fingers and toes, tired of shivering until my teeth chattered. Paul figured it all out, explaining that maybe I would never get used to it, that swimming in ice water might never feel comfortable or enjoyable to me, but at least I could do whatever it took to stay in. It was nothing more, or nothing less, than a mind game. How much pain could I stand? How long could I bear the cold? As long as I thought I could.

I would imagine that there are a fair number of people who wonder: Why would any sane person put herself through such an ordeal? Maybe the crux of the matter is sanity, but I prefer to think not. I could try to explain why I do these things until I am blue in the face, and my dear father, who never learned to swim, would still never understand, thinking that I swim halfway around the world only to annoy him, to rebel, to negate his values. And perhaps in a sense he is right. It is foolish to deny that there is a desire to say, "I have accomplished this. I have swum around Manhattan. I have done something beyond the realm of normal middle-class life, out of the ordinary, unexpected." It becomes a secret source of confidence, a private wellspring of originality. Mostly I think I just wanted to swim the English Channel because it appealed to me, and all the explanations put forth, all the talk about goals and ideals, is just a rationalization for what was, in effect, a whim. It was a dream that caught my fancy as a young child, from which I hadn't awakened. There are those who will never understand why anyone would want to climb Mount Everest or travel to the North Pole if not for fame and fortune, and then there are the rest of us for whom such endeavors seem admirable and courageous only if done for more singular reasons. It's mostly a matter of personality, of quirks and idiosyncrasies, and for these there are no rational explanations, only excuses.

A woman I know swam the English Channel, then around Manhattan in an attempt to become a celebrity, then was never seen in the pool again. She found fame to be fleeting and didn't realize that the joys of swimming would have lasted a lifetime, could have helped her through the rocky times that followed the attention. There are an infinite number of reasons why athletes and adventurers do these things, for themselves and for those they love, but to put oneself through so much to win the attention of strangers is incomprehensible to me.

I don't remember when swimming the English Channel entered my consciousness. It's as if it has always been there, part of who I am, like a family story told so often that it is absorbed into one's personality long after the memory of the event is lost. It's the one swim that everyone knows, that has the weight of history behind it, across a stretch of sea that has brought ruin to countless ships and has changed the shape of nations. The shortest distance across the Channel is 20.6 nautical miles, or 22 land miles, from Dover, England, to Cap Gris Nez, France. I have forgotten so much of my schooling, but not the facts that Captain Matthew Webb was the first man and Gertrude Ederle the first woman to swim across the English Channel.

Paul proudly brought me as a gift from one of his business trips to England a biography of Captain Webb, who crossed the Channel successfully on his second attempt on August 23–24, 1875, staying in the 60-degree water for twenty-one hours and forty-five minutes, slathered with porpoise grease. Considering that Webb swam breaststroke, as few as fifteen strokes a minute, and had a bit of brandy on the way to ease the pain from a jellyfish sting, his time wasn't half bad. It would be another thirty-six years before anyone repeated his feat. Meanwhile, Matthew Webb's life went off-course. It seemed that he became addicted to publicity, swimming long distances and races for fame and fortune, traveling back and forth between the United States and England, wherever there was a dollar or a pound to be made. It was the only way he knew to support his family. He was thirty-five years old when he died in a foolish attempt to swim across the Niagara River, at a terrifying point known as the Whirlpool Rapids. Those who knew the river well tried to dissuade him but he would not listen. He wore the same red silk swim trunks he had worn while crossing the Channel, but what he did in the Niagara River could not be considered swimming. The ferocious waves pounded him into oblivion and his battered body was found eight miles downstream. Engraved on his tombstone in a cemetery in Niagara Falls are the words: "Nothing great is easy." He left a widow and two young children.

The Channel was not swum again until 1911, again by an Englishman, Thomas Burgess, on his twelfth attempt. He had averaged two tries a year since 1904. Then it was another eleven years until the next successful swim. In 1926, an American teenager, Gertrude Ederle, became the first woman to swim the English Channel, and she broke the record as well. She was given a ticker tape parade upon her return to New York City. Within a very few weeks, another woman conquered the Channel, and Ederle's record of fourteen and a half hours did not even last the summer. It was shattered by two hours by a German man. Once records start falling, they are broken, for the most part, with amazing speed. It hurts to swim fast, and there are psychological barriers to pushing oneself beyond certain limits, but once one knows that someone else has accomplished something, it is easier to do it oneself.

J U N E   1 0 ,   1 9 9 0

We spent the better part of a very dark afternoon driving around with the canoe tied to the top of the car, trying to figure out when exactly it was going to rain, attempting to find a new place to swim, even though I prefer to keep to familiar lakes. I am slightly on edge in water I don't know intimately. I judge, and remember, bodies of water by their taste, their feel, their color. Brownish water, in the Adirondacks, is often metallic, from a high iron content, and leaves an unpleasant aftertaste. I swam a ten-mile race once in Candlewood Lake, Connecticut, where the water was hateful for many reasons—too warm, too muddy, too weedy, and worst of all, it tasted of gasoline, from the numerous motorboats. Saltwater on the East Coast is always cloudy, if not downright murky, as in the East River, which makes the sparkling turquoise of the Caribbean a revelation.

We ended up back at comfortable Paradox Lake sometime in the late afternoon, unable to justify any further delay. I told Paul that there was no need to put the canoe in, that he could just sit and read on the beach if he wanted, but the black flies were swarming and he figured they wouldn't follow him over the water. So he took his book, paddled out a way, and let the boat drift while he read and I swam down the shoreline.

Suddenly, instantaneously it seemed, the sky blackened and the wind roared in. I frantically treaded water, pushing myself as high as I could, searching over the waves for Paul. In the seconds it took for the weather to change, I never considered swimming to shore, the obvious choice, but only thought of finding my way back to Paul. I saw him before he saw me, the white canoe being a stronger beacon than my safety orange bathing cap. He was paddling madly, trying to find me. The timing was out of a novel—we were no sooner side by side than the heavens opened, pouring forth torrents of rain. I clung to the bucking canoe and tried to pull myself out of the turbulent water. Then, luckily, sanity hit. I've swum in rain and wind and waves—never in all those conditions in water quite that cold, but I was fine. I yelled as much to Paul; he shouted back that he was okay and to head for shore. I could breathe only on my right side; breathing on my left resulted in mouthfuls of lake water and rain. But somehow I forgot the cold, forgot the fear, and found the exhilaration. Waves often have that effect on me, the way I would imagine wind affects sailors or powder affects skiers. Playfulness overrode any trepidation. I was tossed about like a child being thrown into the air by its father, and responded as lightheartedly, scoffing at any storm that had the gall to try to stop me.

Paul was as wet as I and shivering by the time we reached shore. Unfortunately, there was a problem—it wasn't the intended shore. Our car was still some distance down the lake We talked about stopping anyway and waiting for the weather to calm down but realized that would accomplish nothing. We would still be cold and wet but going nowhere. So we made our respective ways down the shoreline, two bedraggled creatures acting as the punch line to one of nature's jokes. We passed a group of people sitting on their front porch, sheltered under a roof, watching the storm and drinking beer. Afterwards, Paul told me they had commented that it was a nice day to be out on the lake, voices dripping with sarcasm. Yeah, well, we saw the humor, too. The whole day wasted only to end up swimming through the storm we had been attempting to avoid.

The wind diminished and the rain weakened on the way back. Paul pulled ahead of me and by the time he reached the beach the sun was shining and the lake was glass, as if we had made the whole thing up. And when I walked shakily out of the water, Paul was standing there, as trained, holding a sopping beach towel to wrap around me, smiling ruefully at our unfortunate timing.

Weather is the most important variable when swimming the English Channel. Tides can be figured from charts, but gales come seemingly out of nowhere. A forecast for twenty-four hours is essential, to allow for preparation, as well as the actual swim, but predictions don't always come true. Calm seas are rare and do not last long. The prevailing winds tend to be southwesterly, but can change direction precipitately, causing rough water off the coast of France. *The Channel Association Handbook* reads like a weather primer, and includes a map of the water areas which surround the British Isles, all of which are delineated and named, and the Beaufort Wind Scale, so that one can know what numbers signify which wind velocities, and understand the exact difference between, for instance, a "gentle breeze" and a "fresh gale." It includes little tips: a barometer which moves steadily tends to mean settled weather; sudden ups and downs signal unsettled weather. Sometimes low pressure occurs during a fair spell, but it is usually followed by rain and/or wind. A red sky at night does bode well, as does a gray sky in morning, or a dawn that lightens slowly. Red sky at morning is a warning of storms or wind, and a dawn that is first visible high in the sky, above clouds, foretells wind. There is a saying in upstate New York, "If you don't like the weather in the Adirondacks, wait five minutes." Our impression was that the situation was similar on the English Channel, that lurking somewhere behind every golden sunlit minute was a shrieking gale with hurricane-force winds.

I thought I knew a lot about fog, based on years of morning swims, and evenings spent in a valley in Paradox through which water flows. But English Channel fog sounded more complicated, appearing as it did in endless variation. It often serves as a harbinger of changing weather. Certain types of mist cause a choppy sea; others seem to rest on the calmest water. Haze can cause mirages on clear days. When fog enlarges objects, it indicates good weather, but when it causes distortion, rendering known things unrecognizable, rain or wind are on the way. Fog tends to isolate, which isn't all bad, since the escort boat is all that needs to be seen, and it also enhances depth perception because it blurs distant and not so distant objects, sometimes causing that which is nearby, such as a boat, to loom unnaturally large as it is unconsciously compared to what appears to be much farther away, such as land. These optical illusions can be confusing, especially when compounded by goggles and fatigue.

In Paradox, the fog was either there when I awoke or it seeped in slowly on the evening breeze. Near or on the ocean, obscurity can come with frightening speed. One afternoon, when I was younger, I fell asleep on a Cape Cod beach, under a bright midday sun. Shrill whistles awakened me to a world I did not recognize. I rubbed my eyes, frightened by my clouded vision, worried that it was internal, specific to myself, some horrible fast-growing glaucoma, until I recognized the damp chill of a heavy fog. Voices were muffled, floating from the dark, indistinct shapes gathering belongings, warning the smaller shapes not to wander away. The lifeguards had cleared the water, or so they hoped, as it was no longer possible to see the ocean. I sat on my towel for a while, enjoying the strangeness, until I, too, joined the exodus. I found my bicycle and rode immediately up a slight incline into dazzling sunshine, turning back to look into the diaphanous whiteness, to reassure myself that it was not a figment of my imagination.

I returned to the city with Paul. I needed to concentrate on both cold water and distance, and it was easier to put in the miles at the pool. Besides, the past week without him in Paradox had seemed so long. We met when I was thirty years old. I had led a mostly solitary life—no prom dates, no long-term boyfriends. I had lived alone from the age of nineteen. I longed for a close relationship in spite of my strong suspicion that I was unsuited for one. Marriage was not one of my most important goals; it was somewhere below leading an interesting life. I worried that I would feel stifled living in close proximity to another human being, that he would get on my nerves. I thought I was so independent. Little did I expect that when I fell, it would be with the same resounding thud as anyone else who has ever fallen head over heels in love. It was almost frightening, how quickly my life was turned upside down.

I arrived at the New York State Theatre at Lincoln Center one morning in October 1985, to draft the scenery for the opera *Werther*. The set designer was a very dear Belgian friend, and I had spent a week translating for him at production meetings. I was nervous about doing the working drawings after he left, but since I felt vaguely responsible, and somewhat knowledgeable about what he wanted, and had no other work anyway, I agreed to give it a try. So there I was, in the wings stage-right, when the technical director, a college friend, introduced us with a twinkle in his eye. "Sally, this is Paul Carter," he said. "He'll take you downstairs and show you where everything goes."

Okay by me, I thought, double entendre understood and appreciated, and trying not to blush. Certain events seem to have an inevitability in retrospect, but it's probably how we make sense of the inexplicable. I once transferred my family's home movies to videotape and included a sound track. Because I didn't have the equipment at home, I timed the music and the film, put them together, and hoped for the best. I was amazed when certain parts worked out perfectly, when my sisters and I walked through the backyard in our frilly party dresses exactly in sync with the Minuet in G. I discussed this phenomenon with a friend who was a sound designer. He told me that it was actually a trick of the mind, that when one hears music and sees action, the brain matches the two, helps the one sense define the other. Maybe that's all inevitability is, a way of imposing order, of seeing events as if they had a beginning, middle, and end, as if they were meant to happen, as if a life ended too soon was somehow complete.

I thought it perfect that we met in a theatre, offstage, the place where, besides a swimming pool, I felt most at home. We had both made it through our respective high schools by working on stage crew. I, for the first time in my life, learned the satisfaction of building things, of hitting a nail squarely on its head, feeling it sink into the wood without splitting it, the pleasure of running a saw cleanly across a board, and smelling the sawdust that blew into the air behind it. Paul had grown up with these things, and had moved far beyond me in this kind of knowledge, of how things work and how to build complicated stage sets. These were skills that I admired, to which I was attracted, these practical abilities applied to the impractical world of the theatre. We shared an attraction to the performing arts, without any desire to perform. We wanted to do something different, but to be invisible. Unlike the actors, onstage in whatever plumage fit the play or the period, strutting under bright lights in view of the audience, we hid in the shadows, wearing black to allow us to fade into the background. My Belgian friend once said that a performance is like an iceberg, with thirty percent, the actual show, visible, and the other seventy percent, the part that holds it together, makes it happen, hidden beneath the surface, unseen by the audience. One of the most magical experiences in life, for me, will always be to watch a performance from the wings, from underwater.

I have never been able to paint faces. For one of the union exams that I failed, the project was to copy a portrait by John Singer Sargent of a woman dressed in a voluminous gown, reclining on a sofa. The drapery of her skirt, the intricate folds and wrinkles, the light on the satin, all kept me occupied, but her face was torture. I showed the finished product to a scenic artist for whom I was painting murals at the time and he surprised me by saying that her face looked fresh and well done. I thought he was kidding, so convinced was I that anyone would be able to see the extra paint buildup from the countless times I had painted it out and started again. I have an equally difficult time describing Paul's appearance. To describe his features analytically would be somehow to separate out my feelings for him, which I am unable to do. I sometimes wondered if he was handsome to others, or just to me. I felt that I couldn't see him clearly, that I started falling in love the moment I met him and that since I only grew to love him more and more, I never had the chance to judge him impartially, to see him years later and think, Why, yes, he was quite good-looking, or What was I thinking?

Paul was lanky, never having lost the adolescent gawkiness that most teenagers shed as they age. He relished finding gray hairs among the dark brown, wanting to look older, more distinguished, and maybe the mustache was part of that as well, but it was the boyishness that appealed to me. I loved being able to see what I thought of as the boy in the man, which was as much due to a youthful outlook as to looking young. He had such passionate interests in different subjects that I couldn't help but be fascinated. When we met, he had the pallor that came from spending too much time in a dark theatre, his skin unlined from not having been exposed to the aging sun. I felt responsible for his painful bout of sun poisoning the first summer we were together. Years of swimming outside and summers spent lifeguarding had toughened my hide; it took many weekends at Jones Beach and several vacations in the sun, but eventually he caught up. When I think of trying to explain what it was that attracted me to him, I have a recurring image of the kinds of shirts he wore. They were always cotton, button-down, and not the least bit attractive, but they clothed a kind of vulnerability rare among New York's generally more sophisticated or macho men.

Paul told me how he was given a football scholarship to major in theatre—he never touched a football, but the head of the theatre department designed new uniforms for the team and the mysterious deal worked out to his benefit. After college, he worked on some TV movies, some dinner theatre, etc., and decided he needed graduate school to get anywhere. So he took out a student loan and went to Yale, which he described, when asked, as a "technical school in New Haven." I admired this about him, not that he went to an ivy-league school, for the Drama School didn't really count as such, and we both disliked its air of pretentiousness, but that he decided what he wanted to do with his life and even though it was totally out of context in terms of his family, or what he knew from experience, he went out and did it. New York was intriguing that way, for it contained so many people who had come from elsewhere, who believed in the pursuit of dreams, who were driven to escape the comfort of staying somewhere they knew too well. They weren't necessarily any happier than those who stayed behind, but surely the plunge into the unknown counted for something.

Our paths came intriguingly close to crossing before we actually met. He had gone to Madison to investigate the theatre department shortly after I left; later he worked in Pittsburgh, my hometown. I, meanwhile, had moved to New York after a year spent in Europe, traveling and working in French theatres. I began my career planning to be a set and lighting designer, which I did, in minuscule off-off Broadway theatres. Usually I built and painted my own sets, and hung and cabled my own lights. I also worked in numerous theatres as carpenter, electrician, assistant to the set or lighting designer, and stage manager. Over time I was being worn down. I realized that without graduate school I was in a certain rut, but I had no desire to go back to school. Of all the things I did, I thought that painting scenery was what I enjoyed most, and the most reasonable way to make a living, provided I got into the union. I liked the idea of being paid by the hour, going home and leaving my work troubles at work. Designing was too traumatic, too all-encompassing. I didn't want to spend my life inside a dusty theatre toiling away eighty hours a week. I wanted a life outside, to supplement work I enjoyed.

Paul set me up at an empty drafting table, which happened to be adjacent to his, but there was a partition between them. We would blindly toss supplies back and forth when one of us needed something the other had. It was part of the flirtation. Objects as mundane as a roll of masking-tape dots became imbued with romanticism. I asked questions, made up problems with measurements, anything to have an excuse to talk, to entice him to look over my shoulder as I wondered how a particular flat should be constructed. Paul stayed for the performances in the evening, so there was no easy opportunity to go for a beer after work, or even walk out of the theatre together. Instead, I went swimming, and obsessed—what did he think, did he like me, was I just someone he worked with. I finished the drafting and still he hadn't made a move.

I called him at home on some pretext, stealing his phone number from the call sheet posted in the office, and happened to mention that I was thinking about going to see a movie. "What movie?" he asked nonchalantly. I was so relieved, overjoyed, by that simple question, as it allowed for the possibility that he would want to go with me.

The film we saw took place in New York City, mostly in SoHo.

We were in my neighborhood, Chelsea, so after eating dinner at a Mexican restaurant, I walked him to the bus stop at the end of my block, to prolong the evening, and then waited with him for the bus, which came sooner than it ever did when I stood there by myself. I received a peck on the cheek for my trouble, but from that point on, never a day passed without our talking to each other, or at least that's how it seemed. I missed him when I spent that Thanksgiving with my family; he missed me when he spent Christmas with his; and those were the last holidays we spent apart.

I worried that I was far more madly in love than he; his quiet reserve was sometimes hard to read. It was quite a while before I realized that he had cared what I thought, that he had, at least once, tried to impress me. Sometimes, after the Saturday-night performance, he would come over, bringing the Sunday *Times*. I liked to do the crossword puzzle; he couldn't spell and tried to stay away from it. One night, as he sat beside me, I leaning against him, he came up with an obscure British word that fit the spaces. I was amazed and made a big deal of how brilliant he was, how splendid it was that he knew this esoteric scrap of information. He was quite pleased with himself, irresistible in his smugness. Months later, his brother-in-law was in town and we went to see *Brigadoon* at City Opera, where Paul was still working. It was a Thursday evening. Backstage, before the curtain, we were chatting with one of the stagehands when I noticed a copy of the Sunday *Times* magazine section lying open to the crossword puzzle, which was almost completed. "Oh," I said, teasing, "it takes you this long into the week to finish it?"

"No," he replied. "This is next Sunday's. We get the early

sections a few days before." It took me well into the first act to realize that I'd been had, and I still smile over the memory.

We both had strong personalities, and opinions, which we fought over a fair amount. We sensed that nobody could tell us what to do, that we had to figure things out for ourselves, but found that making sense of life with someone at one's side is a world away from doing it alone. It was not always an easy process. The fights scared me until I realized that even though we both became angry, it was a way of working things out, letting off steam, and that what was between us would outlast the spells of bad weather. Over time, the fights decreased. We knew the code words to let each other know we had been there before and it wasn't worth it. In the midst of one argument, Paul had blurted out, "Okay, so I'm a horrible person." Afterwards, when we finished, I laughed and said, "I can't believe you said you're a horrible person."

"I said that?" he asked, not remembering, grinning. It became a catchphrase, a way of forestalling, of admitting wrong. "I'm a horrible person," one of us would say, knowing it would remind the other one of the truth.

We both loved to read; I first became aware that what was between us had gone beyond the "dating" phase one evening when I wasn't feeling well. He came to my apartment and we just sat together and read. It was a special night. I had never felt so comfortable with anyone in my life. It was much better than being alone. Paul preferred nonfiction; I tended toward fiction, but we shared and overlapped, persuading each other at least to look at each other's favorite books. When I was growing up my mother used to claim that the house could burn down around me and I would just sit there reading. In Paul, I met my match. We both had been raised not to read at the table, and mostly we didn't, but every so often one of us would catch the other sneaking glances at a magazine or book sitting on the edge of the kitchen table and the other one would proclaim that it was okay to read just that once as we each grabbed some printed matter and the meal continued in quiet companionship. Neither of us owned a TV set when we met.

Everything seemed to fall into place that year I turned thirty. I was accepted into the union at long last. Paul was in my apartment the evening the phone call came, and we celebrated by drinking champagne at the Lion's Head, a venerable literary bar in the Village. Love and work formed the parameters of my life. My favorite paradox had always been that of solitude: one is far lonelier in a group of people than alone, by oneself. Paul turned that concept inside out. I was lonely only when he wasn't there. Every so often I tried to return to my solitary ways and head upstate by myself, as I always had, but it didn't suit me anymore and I always found myself returning to the city ahead of schedule, eager to surprise him, to turn my key in the lock, open the door, and catch sight of him sitting at the desk, smiling toward me in anticipation.

I moved in with him a year before we married, wary of agreeing to spend my life with someone when I had only lived alone, worried about marriages that broke up within months, or years. I discovered that I needn't have been concerned, that living together strengthened the bonds, reinforced the conviction that I wanted to grow old with this man. I looked forward to the time, some years into the future, when we would have been together long enough so that I no longer missed him whenever we were apart, when I could escape what I thought of facetiously as the "tyranny of love." We were married on May 8, 1988, in a restaurant on the far side of the East River, a site chosen for its proximity to water, at a time late enough in the day that Manhattan became an impossibly beautiful backdrop in the dying light.

The English Channel swim was born out of happiness, out of intoxication with the life I was living. That spring I had the best job I ever had—painting scenery for the movie *Green Card*, directed by Peter Weir, designed by his wife, Wendy. They were a charming couple who set the tone for a lovely experience. Most movies are more drudgery and nonsense than the general public could ever imagine; this one was more art and pleasure than I could ever have dreamed. The film was set in the kind of New York City apartment that only exists in the mind of an Australian art director. It was beautiful but not real, or at least not in life in New York City as I knew it.

The fun of being a scenic artist is in creating histories and personalities for the characters in the film. We read between the lines of the screenplay. We know that the paint buildup is different in a Lower East Side tenement than in a Park Avenue co-op, and that people tend to leave fingerprints around light switches, and that if this character is a slob, he or she will leave coffee-cup rings on the windowsills. This is known as "aging" and it is what makes a movie set look lived in, instead of like rooms in an architectural design magazine. The appeal of this particular apartment for the character was that it had a wonderful greenhouse with walls of small panes of glass and a domed roof, as well as a terrace, giving us a variety of textures and surfaces to re-create.

Usually the director breezes through the set a day or two before rehearsals are scheduled to start, engulfed in a haze of cigar smoke, with an entourage of "suits" who, when they deign to notice our presence, muster as much disdain as possible. Producers count dollars when they see us at work, and wonder why people wearing tattered clothes covered with paint should earn so much, taking money that would be better spent adding lights to their own tennis courts, or which could be used to augment the obscene salary already being paid to some movie star of dubious talent. Peter Weir, on the other hand, was on the set every day, alone or with his cinematographer, to become familiar with the space, to examine the possibilities. He was appreciative of our work, which gave us pleasure, and challenged us. There are reasons that his films look beautiful. Details mattered, and time and care were taken to make the fantasy appear real. We painted moss growing between the fake flagstones on the terrace, re-pointed areas in the plastic brick walls, created water stains in the bathroom ceiling. There was an uncommon amount of laughter and energy on that set.

Every so often, we, the scenic artists, would go for a drink after work. Each time, I called Paul, and he tried to join us, the only spouse in the group to do so. I liked my co-workers, but I preferred Paul's company to anyone's and wanted him to be part of my free time whenever possible. Everyone liked him; he was nice, he was funny, he was interesting, and, as long as we didn't talk about work too much, he enjoyed himself. Actually, he loved hearing about the technical side of the job; it was the gossip about people he didn't know that he found tedious. He missed, in his work as a theatre consultant, being part of a production, with the deadlines of shooting schedules, or opening nights. He liked stories about scenery being loaded onto a truck while the paint was still wet, about mishaps on the film set, about the constant scheduling conflicts brought about by uncooperative weather or missing actors.

Paul had written a book called the *Backstage Handbook*, subtitled *An Illustrated Almanac of Technical Information*. He had been working as a stagehand some years before and had needed to know which pin of a standard stage plug was hot and which was neutral. He searched through several stagecraft books and was surprised when this basic piece of information was nowhere to be found. As time went on, he noticed more little things that were way too difficult to look up. So he started jotting down facts that he had a hard time remembering, things like the strength of ¾-inch manila rope, or how to tie a sheet bend, or how much a sheet of ½-inch plywood weighs. He wanted to put together a booklet that would fit in a stagehand's back pocket but ended up with a book that would fit into a toolbox. It is a wonderful, beautiful book.

The first edition came out the summer after we were married. I was working on a movie, *Last Exit to Brooklyn*, which was being shot in an abandoned warehouse in a rough, gritty section of Brooklyn known as Red Hook. It was steamy inside, broiling outside, and the work was grueling. I was still fairly new in the union and intimidated by all those sweaty men. I mustered up my courage and trudged over to a group of them at coffee break. "This is a book my husband wrote," I said. "You can look at it.

I'm selling it if anyone wants one. I'll come back later"—backing away as quickly as I could. When I went over to the same group at lunch with the half-dozen books I had brought, they started waving money around, grabbing the books, annoyed that there weren't enough, even though I would be back the next day and promised to bring more. I couldn't wait to get home to tell Paul. So eventually, because of the book, more of the guys knew me than would have normally. We tend to be segregated by department, by union.

On *Green Card*, when Paul came to the studio to meet me, I would proudly introduce him to the grips and electricians as my husband the author. They were always gratifyingly impressed, and asked us to autograph their books. Paul signed his name seriously, straightforwardly, I with a lipstick kiss and a giggle. When writing the preface, he had asked for my advice about how to thank people, including myself. I suggested something to the effect of ". . . and of course my incredibly wonderful wife, Sally, without whom none of this would have been possible." He barely rolled his eyes, and wrote instead, at the end of the list of thank-you's, ". . . and of course Li'l Sal," which was, I thought, perfect, except that the nickname was picked up at work, which was embarrassing. It seemed such a personal thing for everyone to know, but when they called me that, it always made me think of Paul and smile.

It was easily the best spring I've ever known. The movie studio was near my health-club pool and I found myself swimming more and more, carried along on the richness of my life, killing time so Paul and I could ride the A-train home together. Friends at the pool started asking if I was training for something and I started thinking: Why not? At thirty-four, I didn't think I could much longer spare the time and concentration needed for a project like the Channel. Swimming around Manhattan was logistically easy. It was, after all, my own backyard, the starting line only a subway ride away.

The English Channel was inconceivable before Paul (B.P. in our shorthand). It was too distant, too costly, too much of a burden to be borne alone. I thought I would do this thing, swim the English Channel, and then start acting like a grownup. Paul had always wanted children. I hadn't. But he brought me around and this is what we would do after the summer, start a family, just like normal adults. I had no sense of a biological clock ticking, no overwhelming attraction to babies. It was a purely personal thing; I wanted to have Paul's child, for him, and believed his assurances that I would love it. The children who drove me crazy were not ours, he reminded me. Paul had this idea, and talked of it, seriously, as if it were possible, never failing to make me laugh. He wanted to invent a serum that would stop the aging process. It would keep puppies small, instead of growing into dogs, and make kittens remain tiny, rather than becoming cats, and enable babies always to be cute, instead of developing into teenagers.

By May I was swimming many thousands of yards a day in the pool, but still we wavered. It would be expensive. It would mean being unemployed for several months, because work started too early to allow me to train with a team, which I felt was necessary. And it would entail spending an entire summer being wet and cold. Then one day I found out that one of my favorite people in the world, Don, was HIV-positive and had been sick. The ambivalence came to an abrupt halt. The sense that life was trickling away was overwhelming, so, to dam the flow, we made the decision to go for it. Swimming is surely an odd way to show one's love, but I dreamed of the day I would return from England and could say to Don, "Here. The better part of this was for you, the part that transcended the physical act of swimming, the part that served as inspiration when nothing less would keep me going."

I knew a man, a wonderful, really fast swimmer, who broke the record for Manhattan Island in honor of his son, who had died in an out-of-the-blue schoolyard accident. He swam with a picture of the boy inside his cap. That same day, while I was breaking the women's record, I was dedicating it, in my mind, to my lighting-design professor, who had died the previous weekend, and who had taught me so much about seeing the world. It is as if we need some greater meaning to endure the intensity of these endeavors, a reason to push ourselves beyond the boundaries of what might be considered normal. But it is also the feeling that this is what we do best, the most we can offer to those we have loved and lost, or are losing.

Don was one of a group of friends I had made through swimming. Because I worked freelance, I met a lot of people and tended to drift in and out of friendships as the jobs came and went. Most of my lasting friendships were made in the pool, and many of them centered on Don. He was the sort of talented and magnetic person who drew interesting people to him. He worked in a studio in an old carriage house in Chelsea, a few blocks from where I then lived. The entrance was through an opening in a large wooden garage door, up a passageway just barely wide enough for a car, and across a cement courtyard.

The lower story was where the horses had been kept; the upper was living quarters. Don rented the downstairs for his design business; someone else lived upstairs. Once a year, in May, Don threw a party, "the barbecue," and the courtyard was packed with friends, odd and fascinating and talented people. At our wedding, Paul said, "This is the perfect party. We walk up to any group of people and they stop talking and turn their attention exclusively to us!" At Don's barbecue, in the years before Paul, I chose to be bartender, which meant nothing more than opening beer bottles, or pouring wine, because then I could talk to everyone without worrying about mingling, or feeling socially inept. Sometimes it felt like the center of the universe, this party, the way bits of my past and future overlapped there.

One year, I found myself staring at a familiar-looking man, blond-haired, blue-eyed, very Nordic, until I remembered how I knew him. He had been in a creative-writing class in college, and the story he wrote, as I recall, was about wolves and snow and cold. I spoke to him, and he remembered my story as well, though it had been many years before. We saw each other only at the barbecue until one year, my first with Paul, he and his wife invited us to a party. The only people we recognized were the ones who looked familiar from the barbecue. We spent most of the evening talking with one couple, Paul describing the book he was in the process of compiling. The man was an artist, and although his theatre background was negligible, he ended up drawing the beautiful illustrations for *The Backstage Handbook*. The chance meetings that change lives, or at least affect them in unexpected ways, were part of the appeal of living in New York.

Another year, my sister was eating breakfast in the Village with a friend, and they could not stop looking at a man at another table. He was the most handsome man they had ever seen, but they figured it was futile; he was too attractive to be straight. That afternoon, when my sister arrived at Don's, there I was, talking to this man, who was a good friend. His name was Rob, he was an attorney and handled the purchase of my house as a favor, for he loved to swim, and was very fast, and spent many weekends in the lakes of the Adirondacks. He never looked where he was going; there were usually three or four of us, and we would say, "Okay, let's swim to that point over there," and Rob would take off, far ahead of us, in the absolutely wrong direction. But he didn't care, so what if he ended up covering twice the distance; the point was the joy of swimming, not arriving at an arbitrary location.

There was a continuous flux to this group of friends. Lovers were added to the group, then they broke away; couples were formed within it, then they separated—until age and AIDS and death froze the tableau into images that exist only in the past. There were lucky ones who married and had children, or were HIV-negative and found love, but there are too many missing for the survivors to ever lose the fear that it would someday happen to them. This wasn't how we imagined growing old back then, not so very long ago.

Don had blond hair, which mostly stood straight up, like a scrub brush, hazel eyes, and a way of smiling, of starting to smile, then straightening his lips, then starting again, then stopping, then finally breaking into the world's most sparkling grin. His lips were forever twitching, ready to curl, to spread from ear to ear. I used to help Don out around the studio, mostly just to be in his orbit, and because there were times when the little he paid me counted for a lot. When my sister called me at the studio and Don answered the phone, she would ask, "Are you smiling, Don?"

"Why does she always ask me that?" he finally wondered.

"Because you have such a great smile. She wants to know, when she imagines what you look like while you're talking, that you're smiling."

Paul used to say that he could always tell when I had spent time with Don because I would pick up his quirky way of grinning. I enjoyed the thought that qualities I liked in my friends rubbed off on me. I was at the pool when a mutual friend gave me the bad news. I didn't want to hear it. "No, no, no," I repeated. "No, it can't be." As if denying what we don't want to hear will ever make it not so. Dripping wet, dripping tears, I ran to the phone in the locker room to call Paul for solace, reassurance. He told me to swim a few laps to get hold of myself, then go home. He would leave work as soon as he could and meet me there. As I hung up the phone, I thought, Thank God I have Paul to get me through this. How could I bear it on my own?

JUNE 17, 1990

We left for what was meant to be two weeks in England and Scotland. My mother, a dentist, had a professional meeting in St. Andrews; Paul's work as a theatre consultant took him to a convention center in Birmingham, and I went along to keep everyone company, knowing there would be no difficulty finding frigid bodies of water in which to swim. Paul stopped working at City Opera about a year after we met. Fearful that he would leave New York, I did all I could to keep him there, talking to friends in the business, searching for leads on employment. He might have found the consulting job through his own connections, they were surely a large part of his being hired, but it was through a friend of mine that we heard about the position. He enjoyed the work, for the most part—figuring out the technical aspects of theatres for new constructions, designing the backstage rigging systems, trying to teach architects about the unique qualities of performance spaces. He traveled to Toronto, to Minneapolis, to Florida, anywhere new theatres were being built. As none of the projects were in New York, he went away fairly often. But this summer he was rarely gone, only a trip or two, and he crammed all his work into one day, maybe two, so, at most, he would spend a single night away. He loved arriving home unexpectedly early, to catch me with a sink full of unwashed dishes, something else to tease me about. He didn't understand why anyone would need more than one plate, one glass, and one set of silverware; I figured if everything still fit under the faucet, it was too soon to waste time washing up.

I spent a few days in Birmingham with Paul, swimming in a dim, old-fashioned pool I had found on a previous visit. Paul was also doing work on a performing-arts center in West Palm Beach, and had discovered that I knew the wife of the man in charge, from college. We had spent time together when they were in New York, and I had traveled to Florida to paint a billboard for the new theatre. They were touring England when we were there, and my friend's husband spent the day on the construction site with Paul while she and I went antiquing. We returned to the trailer at the end of the afternoon, eager to show off our purchases. Paul collected old padlocks, and I had bought two for him, as well as an old book on home carpentry, and for myself, a souvenir pin from Cornwall and an enameled tin cup. He enjoyed the gifts, examined the locks, paged through the book, showed his enthusiasm. My friend's husband was perfunctory, annoyed with something she had bought; it was too big or too heavy. I sensed her jealousy, not so much of Paul as of our shared interests, of how much nicer he was to me than her husband was to her. I am so often uncomfortable when I am with others; I cringe when I see couples treat each other dismissively. I was hurt for her, and glad that even though it might have taken me a long time, I hadn't settled for less than I wanted.

When I asked Paul questions about his friends at work, he didn't seem to know much about them. Like most men, they worked together, and considered each other friends, but were almost complete strangers. "Does this one have a girlfriend?" or, "What does this one's wife do?" and the answer was always "I don't know." Once, when I was laughing at something particularly clever Paul said, I asked him if his co-workers knew how funny he was, how smart, how special. He told me that only I was aware of all these things, the only one who truly knew him. And I thought how important it is to have the person one loves bring out the good qualities, and how we did this for each other, and so were better together than we ever were alone, better at home than at work.

I traveled by train from Birmingham to Scotland to meet my mother. Ironically, after the previous cold-water training, it was the overheated Royal Commonwealth Pool in Edinburgh that did me in, and royally. I hated the 85-degree water but forced myself to do a few miles, sweating all the way, frustrated in my attempts to pass the legions of breaststrokers. It was on the walk back to the hotel that the scratchy throat started; by the next day it was raw and painful. But I decided I couldn't afford to take time off, so my mother and I bustled off to North Berwick, a blustery town on the North Sea. I swam in 53-degree water while she huddled on a bench, clutching my wind-whipped towel, waiting to bundle me into it when I stumbled out, blue and shivering yet again, and more than a little disconcerted by the size of the jellyfish I had seen. There was nowhere to take a hot shower, so surreptitiously, hidden by the towel, I changed back into my dry clothes, reminding myself that being outside in the cold with wet hair doesn't cause illness, germs do. I ignored the fact that the germs had already done their damage. Being cold and wet sealed my fate.

Paul joined us in Edinburgh that weekend, as I continued to train until I was totally without a voice. We spent one night at a quaint whitewashed inn on the banks of bonny Loch Awe, where I had a lovely morning swim in the 54-degree whitecaps. I stayed in longer than planned, reveling in the tingling, stinging feel of my skin. Maybe I was really and truly getting used to the cold! The only blot on an otherwise idyllic swim was the man who rowed over to reprimand me for swimming alone as I scampered out of the water, heading straight for the towel Paul held. We pointed out that there were two spectators standing beside a boat, watching my every move, ready and willing to come to the rescue. He was unappeased but we didn't care, and ignored him as he maneuvered his boat away from the shore, muttering and shaking his head all the while.

I have often thought that one of the rituals at our wedding should have been the "passing of the towel" from my mother to Paul. After all those years she had spent patiently waiting for me on the shore, it was now my husband whom she watched do her job, warmly folding me into the embrace of a towel. Paul and I ran back to our room, where, luckily, there was enough hot water to fill the large tub. I shivered in the steam while Paul worried that I was burning myself as my skin turned red and blotchy. He sat beside me as I soaked until my jaws unclenched and my teeth stopped chattering, talking to me, waiting to bundle me into yet another expanse of terry cloth.

We had rented a car, planning to tour Scotland for a few days and then visit Paul's great-aunt and -uncle in Cornwall. Driving around on the wrong side of the road in the dreary drizzle peering at muddy sheep turned boring quickly. Paul had to do most of the driving, as I am not particularly adept with standard transmission, and his poor right hand was bruised from slamming it into the car door every time he went to shift.

We escorted my mother onto the night train to London, then stood outside her window, waiting for it to leave. Paul had placed some pennies on the track; not only were we there to keep my mother company, we wanted our smashed bits of copper. Paul said to me, "Next time your mother looks up, wave, and move your feet like this," showing me a toe-to-toe, heel-to-heel sliding motion, "and she'll think the train is moving." So when she next glanced at us to see if we were still there, we waved and glided. Night had fallen, she was bent over her suitcase in the square of light framed by the window, and stood abruptly to wave goodbye. When we were beyond her sight line, we stopped and Paul said, "Quick, back the other way," and we slid back into her vision the same way. She was doubled over in laughter, tears in her eyes, arms wrapped around her stomach. The train left, we retrieved our coins, saving one to send to my mother, and returned to the bed-and-breakfast we had found earlier.

Paul and I huddled in bed listening to the rain slap the windows of our bleak, damp, water-stained room, discussing where we wanted to go next. Being the traveler in the family, I decided that it was my responsibility to suggest that we cut our trip short and go home. Paul couldn't have been happier. Love had blunted my wanderlust, clipped my wings, but so gently that I gave in gracefully. There were journeys more subtle, and rewarding, than those to foreign lands. Training was more than a little tedious by then, so any respite, even the two days it would take to return to New York, was a liberating treat. We giggled like two children who were getting away with something, like playing hooky from school. Frankly, after several trips to Great Britain, we were willing truants. We were always cold there, and hungry.

Paul's grandfather Herbert had emigrated from Cornwall when he was sixteen. Before this, he had broken his arm while working in a mine near Porthtowan, and the doctor set his arm wrong, so they had to do it again, but he couldn't, or didn't want to, return to the mine. His mother, Paul's great-grandmother, had a brother in America, who wrote that he could find good jobs for Herbert and his brother Harold if they came over.

So they went, but their parents always regretted it, for Herbert never returned home, and his sister, Paul's Great-Aunt Mildred, never met her brother. The distances Paul's family kept always amazed me, the fact that months would go by, and longer, without their speaking. Maybe it was genetic, this need to separate, to go as far away as possible. Paul's older brother emigrated to Australia, where he married, and settled, and died. Paul's younger brother was living in Germany when we met, and he married there, although eventually he moved back to the States with his wife, and then she returned to Europe without him or her young son, whom she has not seen in many years. The Carters were like pebbles tossed into distant lakes, farther, and farther, until the ripples ceased to intersect, until all they had in common was distance. The womenfolk tended to stay put, and write, so that it was Paul's mother who, although not the blood relative, kept in touch with Aunt Mildred, her father-in-law's sister, and it was Herbert's wife, Pauline, who corresponded with her husband's mother, and I who exchanged letters with Aunt Mildred.

Paul, when he started traveling to England on business, became curious about his grandfather's siblings who lived there. So on one trip, when I had gone along, we wrote to Aunt Mildred, and went off to Redruth to meet her and Uncle Edgar. We didn't know what to expect, whether the English of her letters sounded odd because it was foreign, or if we were in for a bizarre adventure, as family visits so often turn out to be, even when they're not with complete strangers. We took a taxi from the train station, stopping at a house named Cedreka, one in a row of similar houses on a road that sloped down to the rolling farmland just beyond the town. Aunt Mildred, who had been sitting in the front window, waiting, ran out to greet us, a wizened, cheery elf, so excited, grabbing our suitcases to rush us inside, touching us to make sure we were real. Uncle Edgar was large and silent, but equally pleased.

It was February, and we hadn't fully realized what a lack of central heating actually meant, but we were quickly led down an icy hallway into the toasty kitchen, seated next to the coal stove, and offered fragrant, flaky Cornish pasties. We could barely understand them or they us, but that was half the fun. They told us the story of their life together, how they had grown up on neighboring farms. Aunt Mildred, although she had visited America, never lived anywhere else, eventually caring for her elderly parents, as did Uncle Edgar, who had never been farther than thirty miles from the house where he was born, for he had a great fear of heights, so he wouldn't fly, or even climb to the top of a hill. They married when they were fifty, and absolutely, or so it seemed by the looks that passed between them and the easy affection, enjoyed each other's company. We visited other Carters during the day, drinking endless cups of tea in chilly living rooms, searching for resemblances to relatives in America, and played board games at night. Uncle Edgar, though he had not finished high school, beat me at Scrabble, while Paul, accustomed to losing, cheered him on.

We weren't yet married, but on our arrival, Aunt Mildred asked if we wanted to sleep in the same room, it was fine with them, they knew how things were. We hadn't been allowed to stay together at Paul's parents', or at mine, before we were officially wed, yet here we were in this small town, in the home of distant relatives, accepted for what we were. Or maybe it was that they knew how impossible it would have been to achieve any small degree of comfort without the body heat of another, as there was only a small space heater in our room, which we turned off the second before we dove under the covers, to conserve electricity, and we shivered, giggling and whispering, as we wound ourselves around each other, holding on for dear life, seeking warmth.

Aunt Mildred and I shed some tears when we left, the men remained stoic, and we promised to visit again before too long. So it was with considerable regret that we left England this time without seeing Aunt Mildred and Uncle Edgar. We talked of bailing out of Scotland and going straight to Cornwall to visit them before returning to New York, but they were elderly and in poor health by then, so we didn't want to endanger them with my germs. And since I could only whisper at best, it didn't seem as if it would be much of a visit. We decided that nothing was going to keep us from the Channel at this point, so we would see them then, and we tried to bury our regret. Paul worried, "What if one of us gets hit by a bus and we don't make it over in August?" I superstitiously hushed him and said we'd both have to be extra-careful when crossing the street.

J U L Y   4 ,   1 9 9 0

We took the extra vacation time Paul had from cutting the trip to Scotland short and spent some of it upstate. worked freelance; that is, I could choose not to work as much as I pleased. I've had only one full-time, five-day-a-week, year-round job in my life. I lasted about a year and a half, finding it too rigid, too confining, even though the work was enjoyable. I preferred the ups and downs of freelance life, the freedom and the constant changes in rhythm as deadlines approached and were met, the layoffs that followed the intense pressures. I had worked this way long enough that I no longer worried that each job was my last, although that is the common joke among those of us who have chosen this seemingly precarious way of earning a living. Paul had a more structured schedule. We carefully rationed his days off in order to be able to wait as long as necessary in England for optimum tides and weather. We had decided that in his upcoming salary negotiations he would ask for more vacation time instead of a raise, our days spent together being worth more than the money.

In the early evening of the Fourth we went to our friend Lottie's house. She had been widowed several years before I met her and spent her summers on the lake, as she and her husband, he a teacher and she a school librarian, had done all their life together. The rambling wooden house had been an inn. Bedrooms and bathrooms sprawled around an impressive two-story great room with a massive stone fireplace. It was always dark and cool inside, so people mostly congregated on the back deck, which rested on stilts high over the hill that fell away steeply to the lake. Lottie had four grown sons and many friends, so there were always crowds, mostly people I didn't remember.

Two summers before, I had met a woman on this deck, a teacher who worked at the same school as Lottie. She was several years younger than I, tall, blond, and beautiful. I didn't talk to her for very long that I recall, but I recognized her the next summer, the year before this one. Paul and I were standing on the lawn below the deck. Squinting up into the bright sun, I thought I saw her, and asked one of Lottie's sons who was with us, "Is that Heather?" He said that it was and then told us that her husband, to whom she had been married for slightly less than two years, had died the previous winter, of a heart attack, at the age of thirty-five. My breath caught in my throat, a chill raised the hair on my arms, my eyes filled with tears. I grabbed Paul's hand tight in mine, thinking, How can she bear it?, certain that I would be unable to, and yet there she was, sitting in the sun, talking to someone, looking, from this distance, as she always had. I didn't know what to say and do not remember if I spoke to her.

This year the deck was once again crowded with people, mostly couples, and Heather was not there. We all made our way down to the lake for the yearly explosive festivities. On a float, just out from the shore, was a "rocket" made from a six-foot length of Sono tube packed with something to make it blow up. I sat on the hillside next to Paul. As the countdown started, I worried, Are we far enough away? What if it comes straight at us? Paul, laughing, rolled his eyes. I always worried about the wrong things at the wrong times. The fuse was lit, the flame traveled to the rocket, there was an explosion, then smoke, then the rocket rose at least a foot straight up into the air before falling sideways into the water.

We drove into the town of Schroon Lake to check out the official fireworks. They were still hours away but the hillside with the best view was already packed and the mosquitoes were fierce, so we decided to spend a quiet evening at home. As we were falling asleep I noticed the sky brightening and darkening, as if lights were flickering on and off, but we were too far away to be able to see fireworks and the only noise was the ruckus of the frogs and the incessant chant of the whippoorwill. I slid out of bed to look out the window and was treated to an amazing show of heat lightning, electricity arcing across the sky. My skin tingled from the power, from the delicious fear. "Paul," I whispered, awestruck, "come here. You have to see this! It's incredible."

"What is it," he asked, drowsy, half asleep. I described it for him. "I'm sorry," he said. "It sounds wonderful and I know I should come see, but I'm too tired to get out of bed." I stayed up watching, enthralled, as he fell asleep behind me. As I trained more and more, I slept less and less. It was as if I was in a constant state of high energy, always primed, ready to swim. Even at the end of a long day, the exhaustion was a veneer over the vitality.

We had decided that a ten-hour swim should be part of the training, assuming that the English Channel would take about that long, plus or minus an hour or so. There would be little sense of progress in terms of distance, only in terms of time. Each hour would be the limit of my focus, a doubling of the half-hour increments that had led me through Schroon Lake. Short-term goals make feats of endurance possible, be they landmarks or minutes. While swimming around Manhattan, I told myself: Just make it to the Hudson River. Okay, now just get to the George Washington Bridge. Okay, now Riverside Church, now the Empire State Building. To approach it as one massive endeavor would be overwhelming, so one breaks it down into what one imagines to be manageable components.

Unfortunately, we had run out of cold water in the Adirondacks. Everything is, of course, relative, and most people, including my husband, still found the water too excruciatingly chilly for anything more than a brief dip. We chose Lake George, a thirty-mile-long lake, knowing it to be the coldest water close at hand. Having rented a motorboat and drafting a friend, Gregg, to help, we set off at 8 a.m. for a 6 p.m. finish. We waited for the temperature to drop as the hours passed, but it never went below 68 degrees. Even though this was several degrees warmer than anything I was likely to encounter in the Channel, I wasn't exactly sweating, but I knew I had swum in water this temperature for eleven hours when training for Manhattan seven years earlier. So I wasn't suffering as I had in Schroon Lake, or, more accurately, the nature of the pain had changed. Now that I wasn't preoccupied with the agony of freezing, other problems surfaced.

I had forgotten how much it hurts to swim for hours on end. First one shoulder aches, then a leg or an elbow, then the neck, as the pain travels around, seeking the vulnerable spot that might end this nonsense. It was the remnants of Scotland that proved to be the chink in the armor this time. I still had a sore throat, but it hadn't seemed to be a problem until it was too late. The fits started about three hours into the swim. I treaded water, coughing and gagging, until I almost vomited, and then continued swimming. These attacks became more and more frequent. I knew it was at least as painful for Paul to watch from the boat as it was for me. He didn't know if he should try to stop me or let me continue, but quitting was no longer a viable option as far as I was concerned. Finally he searched the pockets of my sweats and found lozenges that I had forgotten. They worked miraculously to soothe my raspy throat, but swimming with one in my mouth was more than I could handle, worse than walking and chewing gum at the same time. I had to try to suck on the lozenge between breaths, then shift it to the side of my mouth to breathe, then back again until the next breath, only seconds away. This sequence proved too much and I ended up chewing the lozenge every time. We rationed those precious things, making them last until the ninth hour, at which point I was home free.

The bond between a marathon swimmer and a support crew is tight. I swim freestyle, or crawl, stroking about seventy-two times a minute. I alternate-breathe—that is, I breathe on my left, take three strokes, then breathe on my right, take three strokes, etc. Therefore, I am looking at my boat every six strokes, or a dozen times a minute, or seven hundred and twenty times an hour. All the quick glances add up to a long stare, the way flickering images make an old movie or barely noticed gestures become memory. Sometimes the difficulty in focusing my eyes is frustrating. I think I have seen something on one breath; by the next, the picture will have changed, leaving me uncertain as to what is real and what is imagined.

The second time I swam around Manhattan, it was obvious to me that the support crew on the boat was having a great time and their exuberance spilled over into the water. They cheered every time we went under a bridge on the Harlem River, every time we passed a recognizable landmark, rejoicing in tandem with me, providing the inspiration I needed to break the women's record. I knew which friends were really keyed into the swim and which ones were sneaking beers or working on their tans. And then there were those countless swims through rain and dark—surely more numerous than those through sunlight. There is nothing more discouraging than watching a friend bundled up, huddling under a newspaper in a futile attempt to stay dry, knowing that I, and I alone, am responsible for his or her discomfort and boredom. It reached the point where my closest friends declined offers of all-expenses-paid weekends in the Adirondacks. Training with Paul allowed me to rid myself of the guilt for the most part. We were too intertwined to allocate responsibility or blame—even to remember whose idea the whole thing was. Training together added romance to the tedium, another layer to the pattern of our life. In earlier years I had hated the intrusion of a boat; the summer of the English Channel, I hated swimming alone.

The Lake George swim lasted a little over ten hours because the water was too choppy for me to climb into the boat easily and, besides, Paul could see a beach with a dock in the distance and wouldn't it be more fun if I walked out of the water and pretended it was France? (We didn't finish at our starting point, having chosen to swim six hours down and four hours back in search of cooler, deeper water.) There is nothing so solid and sure as ground beneath one's feet after ten hours spent prone, floating on drifting liquid that slips away if I let it, that adapts to my shape. It was a slow ride home, as the waves were too big to push the boat very hard. Gregg took the helm. Paul covered me with towels and blankets and used his body to shield me from the wind, all the while grinning with pride and excitement. After the boat, and after the car ride home, and after the long, hot shower, the floor continued to roll as the room spun slowly around me, as if the churning water were still jostling me, as if I weren't actually standing, firmly planted, in the safety of our own home.

The rest of July was spent in a tightly scheduled training regime. I left the apartment every morning before six o'clock for a workout in the fifty-meter outdoor pool at Roberto Clemente State Park in the Bronx. It was a bittersweet pleasure training in a place named for one of my childhood heroes. I may have grown up swimming, but my sports idol was a right fielder whose skill and grace were matched by his kindness and generosity. I was in Puerto Rico with my family when his plane crashed into the sea. I spent hours on the beach staring toward the horizon, hoping to spot him floating on a bit of wreckage, wanting so badly to have the chance to swim out to save him.

Swimming in a pool after lakes or oceans feels like child's play. The water takes on the color of the smooth aqua walls, invariably the same, instead of changing from celadon to raw umber to midnight blue. The surface is never opaque, never confused by reflections. The bottom is always visible, the ends always within reach, no more than a few strokes away. Distances are precisely measured; swimming the shortest distance from one end to the other is as simple as following the line clearly painted on the bottom. The water feels lighter in consistency, easier to pull through. There can be a bit of chop if there's a thrasher nearby, but the nonturbulent lane dividers quickly tame the surface. The temperature is almost always too warm for me, although the people without enough body fat complain, shivering, that it is too cold.

When I started working out in New York, my teammates swam in Masters meets. It was, theoretically, the reason for training. I assumed that since I was an adult, I would be able to put all those childhood fears behind me, have fun at competitions, and swim fast. I was wrong. I still couldn't sleep the night before, could barely force down breakfast, continued to spend the day with a very queasy stomach. My meet times were far too similar to my workout times; starting from a dive should have counted for more. I watched teammates who day after day were my exact speed race past me the day of a meet.

One night before a meet, I went out to dinner with some of those friends, to carbo-load, although I had no appetite. Returning to my apartment and seeing the flashing light on my answering machine, I found myself hoping for a message that would allow me to back out of swimming the meet, that something important, overriding, would happen, so that I would have an excuse. I pushed the playback button and heard my mother's tearful voice. My grandmother had died. I flew to Pittsburgh the next morning. For the second time in my life, I decided, enough, no more swim meets.

I chose to stick to what I loved best, swimming competitively at daily workouts. The race was against the clock, and one's teammates. We did "interval training," sets of various lengths done in varying amounts of time. Paul laughed when I said things like, "We did ten four-hundreds on six today." It's like a foreign language to those who don't know. So I explained to him—it meant that we had done sixteen lengths every six minutes, repeated ten times. He would ask me how I picked up the bits of information I relayed to him, how we had time to talk when we were supposed to be swimming. He didn't realize that six minutes left a fair amount of time at the end if I swam fast enough. Since the interval was set, our rest is varied by the speed with which we swim. If we are too slow, and barely make the time, the next interval is harder, and harder, as the second hand on the pace clock seems to spin out of control. Not making the time is embarrassing and discouraging. If one is barely touching the wall before pushing off to go again, the seconds speed by; if one is swimming well, and the interval is generous, the seconds of rest seem to last forever. When friends work out together, conversations are held in those seconds, lives exchanged. Often the time swimming is spent thinking about what was just said, and how to respond. In some ways it is the perfect way to carry on a conversation; words are spoken quickly, but not in haste. Editing occurs in the lengths between sentences.

Workouts are structured with a beginning, middle, and end. I rarely do more than rudimentary stretching, preferring to loosen up in the water by swimming slowly. Having swum both morning and evening workouts, I find that it is much easier to warm up in the morning. Still half asleep, groggy, I slide easily through the water in the early hours of the day. By evening, after hours of physical labor, my muscles are tensed into bundles of aches and pains. Troweling cement, manipulating long roller poles, scrambling up and down scaffolding—all these activities take their toll. There are times when I'm not comfortable in the water until long past the warm-up, when the workout is almost over; other times, I never feel right, my shoulders remain too tight to be strong. More often than not, however, when I see the second hand on the pace clock sweeping past the numbers, some fundamental energy within me kicks in, and I push off the wall in a burst, swimming for all I'm worth.

Individual coaches mix up workouts differently. I prefer workouts with some cohesion, which lead from one set into another in a way that makes sense. There are sets in which we slow our time by two seconds, then speed it up by three, and so on. It is surprising how concrete a second can be, how I can know exactly what three seconds faster over four lengths feels like. It's not easy to make up constantly interesting workouts, and more often than not, there is a certain predictability, which is fine. Sometimes nothing feels so right as a comfortable rut—four-hundreds followed by two-hundreds followed by one-hundreds, especially because within the familiar there is so much room to grow. The goal in any set is not just to make the interval but to negative-split it, to swim the last four-hundred faster than the first. In a set of, say, five four-hundreds, anything after the third one is "downhill." The term may be irrational, because water seeks its own level, but it is apt, if only for psychological reasons. And within each four-hundred, we try to swim each successive hundred faster than the previous one. At the very end, we struggle to "bring it home," to swim the last twenty-five yards the fastest of all. This seems to go against the natural order of things, whereby life winds down slowly, and fatigue accumulates. Instead, we are expected to give our best effort when we are most tired, to go out in a blaze of energy, to show that there is something left at the end.

Sprints usually finish off a workout. The only good thing about sprints, to me, is that they are, by their very nature, short. My problem is that I'm barely getting started and then they're over, then a brief rest, just enough to let the muscles tense, then it's time to go again, but not long enough to have it feel right. The most punishing end to a workout I remember, and one I've never been inclined to repeat, lasted only the length of the pool, twenty-five yards. Actually, it was swum in a fifty-meter pool, so it was the width, and therefore looked even shorter. We were ordered to expel all the oxygen in our lungs, and then to sprint the twenty-five yards without breathing. Never has a short distance seemed so long; lungs burning, lactic acid paralyzing, arms thrashing, we all made it to the other side then gasped giant gulps of air, which hurt just as much as lacking it. Someone next to me panted, "I don't think this is very good for us." The understatement made me laugh. For those who cheated, and snuck a breath, the punishment was fifty yards of fly. Coaches are omniscient, and obeyed.

Sometimes, when people ask why I swim as much as I do, I reply, "Because it feels so good when I stop," which may sound perverse, but it has a physiological basis, having to do with the production of endorphins. I am absolutely energized after a workout, my body glows through the aches, the blissful fatigue washes away my cares. It is an addictive feeling. There is no shortcut to achieving it; the only way is swimming through a tough workout, putting everything into it, and somehow coming out on the other side the better for the effort.

I had worked out with two teams over the years—one at my health-club pool, the other, which was generally referred to as the City College team in the winter, and the Clemente Manta Ray Swim Team in the summer. It was made up of a few age-group swimmers (high school), the actual college team, and Masters swimmers; that is, anyone over twenty-five. I truly loved being part of this group. When we went to Puerto Rico to train at Christmas break in a fifty-meter outdoor pool, college teams were there from all over the United States, and they looked like a different species—tall, tanned, musclebound gods and goddesses with chlorine-bleached hair, amazingly homogeneous, while we, the City College team, were a vast range of shapes and sizes and colors and ages. Paul used to say that the great thing about families was that you came to know people you had nothing in common with. Swim team was like that, too. My friends ranged from a world-renowned, immeasurably kind ophthalmologist to the best-looking state trooper in New York City to a casting director who once got me a role in a "real people" commercial. Swimming was the common bond, speed the common goal, and respect was accorded more to times than to professions or income.

There was a woman who used to work at the health-club pool as a lifeguard and train with the same team as I. She was one of the fastest swimmers I ever knew, did the most beautiful butterfly I had ever seen, and could kick as fast without fins as I kicked with them. For a long time I was intimidated by her, assuming her to be aggressive and overbearing. We became friends. She turned out to be one of the sweetest, nicest people I've ever met, which taught me that swimming fast is nothing more than swimming fast. It's enough sometimes, but it's not a character trait. I have learned not to judge athletes by mere physical prowess, or actors by their roles, or celebrities by their fame. Instead, in the pool, I judge those I don't know by their lane etiquette, by whether they're there to swim or to prove something. Most people who train in a group understand the value of working with one's teammates, the pleasure in having those of similar speed, or better yet, faster, but not too much faster, to spur one on.

The summer of the Channel, I swam a lot with a friend, Brian, who was at the time training to swim around Manhattan. Paul used to come to workouts on weekend mornings, so we could go straight from Clemente to Jones Beach. He would watch workouts but, not being a swimmer, didn't necessarily understand the protocol, or the strategy. Brian and I were about the same speed over the long haul, even though he left me in the dust on a sprint. I came out ahead in the one fifteen-hundred (mile) we did together against the clock, but barely. We were the perfect training partners—I knew he would get away if I slacked off; he knew he'd be in better shape if he let me set the pace. This particular morning, we were swimming a set of two-hundreds—four lengths of the fifty-meter pool. Brian was leading off. I gave him ten seconds, then I went. I caught him by the first hundred meters, coasted behind him for the second hundred. As soon as Brian pushed off the next time, Paul started yelling, "Pass him! Why didn't you pass him?" Instead, I gave him more time, but caught him anyway. Paul was walking alongside the pool, waving his arms, wanting me to pass. Brian knew I had caught him, so, at the end of that two-hundred, offered to let me go first. I declined, told him he should just pick it up.

We both laughed, knowing how tricky it was to swim behind someone of the same speed. Side by side is more difficult, more competitive, but fairer. The principle of drafting carries the follower along. Just as in bicycle racing, it is much more difficult to go first, and a breeze to go second. Even though it felt too slow to swim second, I opted out of the pressure of swimming first, knowing that if I did, Brian would be on my heels, as I had been on his, and I would rather have my goals ahead of me than threatening me from behind.

Workout was over sometime after 8 a.m. I showered away the chlorine, put on a dry swimsuit, shorts, and a T-shirt, and drove out to Jones Beach, arriving around 9:30 most days. I read *The New York Times* as best I could, battling the constant wind, until I could force myself back into the water. Every so often, while in a lake, I was overcome by the "creepy crawlies," possessed of an almost overwhelming fear that some Loch Ness-like monster would rise from the depths and drag me under. I calmed myself by thinking that such a creature would surely recognize me as a kindred spirit and let me be. This worked well enough in a lake, but the ocean was a whole different kettle of fish. The sea was home to creatures far bigger than I, and even the smaller varieties of marine life were capable of inflicting great pain. And then there was the water, overwhelming in its strength, oblivious to any obstacles in its path. The waves mesmerized me with their relentless struggle to free themselves from this world, as they repeatedly fell in on themselves, crashing to the earth in seething failure. There was a friend of mine, a good swimmer and a strong young man, who was tossed into the sand by such a wave and will never walk again, or use his arms. With this always in my thoughts, I watched and waited patiently, painstakingly choosing my moment to burst through the breaking waves, thinking, Please don't paralyze me, please just let me be. Wanting my relationship with the sea to remain superficial, I was determined, with all due respect, to remain on the surface.

One day, after spending what felt like hours reaching for the courage to brave the wall of water pounding furiously before me, I called Paul at work, trembling, almost in tears, to tell him that I didn't think I could do it, I was too scared. "That's all right," he reassured me. "Just drive back into town, do a long workout at the health club, and I'll meet you for dinner." He was much kinder to me than I was to myself.

My daily Jones Beach schedule was to start with a two-hour swim in the ocean. But, like all best-laid plans, it rarely turned out as anticipated, thanks to the capricious mix of tides and currents and wind. Sometimes an hour swum down the beach became a half-hour return trip. At other times it was an hour and twenty minutes back. One day the water would be 68 degrees, the next day 62 degrees. Once I made it past the surf and settled into the saltwater, it was fine. I grew used to its sting, accustomed to the momentary panic I felt when confronted by that surging power. The corklike buoyancy one has in saltwater added to my impression of insubstantiality, allowing me to escape gravity, to experience the grace of weightlessness.

After my two hours, or however long it happened to be, I ate lunch, rested, then swam for at least another hour. Then I showered away the salt, changed clothes again, drove home and waited for the sound of Paul's key in the lock, the lovely, substantial click that signaled the end of a day spent in the isolation of amorphous splashing. Sensory deprivation had taught me to do without a Walkman, to turn my thoughts into a sound track for my life. In my mind I always sang on key, my French was without accent, my conversations sharp and witty. Those fantasies pale to nothingness when compared with the small talk that took place over the dinner table, or while we were lying in bed. The reality was better than the daydream, because of the element of surprise, the spontaneity, the fact that I could never predict what Paul would say, or add to my life.

Weekends were my favorite; I swam the same distance, but it didn't feel as solitary with Paul walking along the shore. Every so often I thought I caught a glimpse of him through the crowds, but mostly I just knew he was there, felt his presence amid the hundreds of people who meant nothing to me. One Saturday or Sunday, I was swimming along, lost in a daydream, not paying attention to anything beyond my thoughts, when I realized that I had been carried, or had swum, very far from shore. There were brief periods of time between swells when I could not see the beach. I adjusted my angle, tried to veer toward the shore, but it never seemed to come any closer. With a little bit of anxiety, I changed my tactic and turned, so that I would swim straight in, just to ease my mind. Eventually the people grew larger, the sand came closer, and I relaxed and resumed swimming parallel to the beach. When I walked out to where Paul was waiting at the end, I asked him if it hadn't seemed that I was pretty far out there for a while. He said he had noticed and started to worry, but then he saw me change course and swim in, and besides, he had often been instructed not to worry; as long as I was in water, I was fine. I was relieved, although I wouldn't admit it, secure in knowing that he was looking out for me, and had been aware when the slightest problem occurred.

During breaks, lying at his side looking enviously at sunbathers baking while I shivered, I would say, "I can't wait for the day when we can just go to the beach and relax. When I don't have to swim if I don't want to. When I can enjoy watching the waves without thinking that pretty soon I'll have to force myself back in." And he would allow me a little bit of extra time before urging me back into the sea.

July drifted by, one day floating into the next, sweeping us along on undercurrents of hope, on the promise of dreams realized. It seemed so simple and childlike—the belief that one could do anything if one just set one's mind to it. That's what I had been taught, what I had been led to believe. As an adult I had come to realize that there were complications, that giving one's all wasn't always enough, but that summer I regressed into all those youthful assumptions. That tantalizing goal wove its seductive web around us and we were always just a little excited, slightly exhilarated, and overwhelmingly in love. I was old enough to fear that it was too good to be true, too good to last. Or maybe that's just how I remember it, looking back through watered-down memories.

 Thursday started off quietly enough. Paul and I slept in until 6:30 and went off to breakfast. I had tossed and turned fitfully the night before but was too excited to be tired.

Today I was going to draw the line between Long Island Sound and the Atlantic Ocean by becoming the first person to swim from Montauk, at the tip of Long Island, to Watch Hill, Rhode Island. It wasn't as if legions had tried, but still, first is first. The swim had been set up for another swimmer, who dropped out because of a shoulder injury. We decided it was a perfect training swim, and if for some reason, such as bad weather, or the unavailability of a boat, I was unable to complete a Channel crossing, I would still have an honorable swim to show for all my training. The currents, temperature, and distance were comparable for the two bodies of water. We worried that the two weeks left before our departure for England might not be enough recovery time, but it seemed too good an opportunity to pass by.

I picked Paul up after work Wednesday afternoon and we sweltered through the rush-hour traffic to Long Island. How could people stand to do this every day, we wondered as we struggled to find open road. We shed more and more cars as we made our way through Long Island, and picked up speed. When we stepped out of the car at the motel, I sniffed the air, like an animal taking measure of its surroundings. The tang of salt boosted my adrenaline, the same way that chlorine does. Since there was a small pool at the motel, I was treated to a blend of two of my favorite scents.

We had dinner in a crowded seaside restaurant. I had pasta, for the carbohydrates, with seafood in it, because one is what one eats. I had dressed up for the occasion. As we left the restaurant Paul said to me, quietly, "You know, I was looking around the restaurant tonight, and you were the most beautiful woman there." I laughed, gratified, knowing that he was not an

impartial observer, but also knowing that it didn't matter anymore if anyone else found me attractive or not. I've never had
a clear picture of what I look like. Sometimes I'll be thinking
that I look pretty good, and then I'll catch a glimpse of myself
in a mirror and wish I hadn't looked, my illusions shattered. In
my years with Paul, I was content with my physical appearance.
He teased me: why didn't I wear clothes that were the right size,
I looked like a bag lady. After many years in a business domi-
nated by men, I felt more comfortable in the burlap-sack look,
hiding my body, feeling self-conscious anyway when I walked
across a stage, the only woman around. At a pool, because I leave
my contact lenses or glasses in the locker room, I can't see, and
therefore feel protected, invisible, oblivious to what others view.

The organizer of the swim had arranged to have it videotaped,
so Paul and I became movie stars for a day. Neither of us shone
in front of the camera, me face down in the water and Paul
retching and wretched. But that's later. It started with us breez-
ily doing our Julia Child imitations. We pureed peaches and
bananas, whipped up a gallon of hot chocolate, poured it all into
thermoses and Tupperware, then packed it into a cooler. We
used a paint stir-stick to mix the food and then used it later to
combine the lanolin and Vaseline with which I grease up. I liked
using painting tools on swims, to try to integrate the disparate
facets of my life, blending a little art into the adventure. The
paint-spattered sports watch Paul used to time the swim was the
same one I wore for work. Lap times may be unnecessary on the
job, but who needs more than one watch that can function after
being submerged in water? At work we use bamboos to extend
the handles of paintbrushes so we can paint a backdrop stapled
to the floor while we stand, to save our knees, but also to give

us some distance from the work. I used these same bamboos, colorful smears and all, as feeding sticks, with a commuter cup attached to the end. Unfortunately, we had forgotten the bamboos in Paradox and had to rig up a shuffleboard pole, which worked so well that we tracked down a telescoping one to take to England. We were very proud of ourselves for having found a feeding stick that fit into a suitcase.

This was the first time I greased up all summer, which signified to me that, after hundreds of miles of swimming, this was the first time it counted. Earlier, I had striven to become inured to the cold. I wanted nothing that would make it any easier at that point. The more difficult the training, the better shot one has when it counts. No one really knows if grease helps preserve body heat, or if it's another trick of the mind, but it was one of my rituals. Now that I was faced with a "real" swim, I was willing to take any edge I could.

As more and more people asked me about sharks, I began to think maybe I should reconsider the glib answers and worry a bit, instead. We couldn't help but notice the many stuffed sharks used to advertise fishing boats. They were far larger than I and seemed to have an infinite number of razor-sharp teeth, but they looked unreal. Death had stolen their power to inspire fear, leaving only their power to inspire. Anyway, it was too late to quit, so I pushed the sharks to the back of my mind, where they conveniently stayed. Some swims through shark-infested waters are done with the swimmer in a cage, others with a sharpshooter on the boat. Both of these precautions seemed too exaggerated given the situation and, though I hadn't done any research into documented attacks, uncalled for.

On the boat ride out to the lighthouse, I asked the captain

of the larger boat, whom I had never met before but who was familiar with this stretch of water, about the risk of sharks. He chuckled and asked where the lady was who would be swimming. I said it was I, and wondered what he found so amusing about shark questions. He shook my hand and said I had about as much of a chance of running into a shark as I had of being struck by lightning. Somehow those odds reassured me, even though I ignored them when buying lottery tickets. I didn't realize that when one is caught in a long shot, the odds skyrocket to a hundred percent, and the law of averages is totally meaningless.

The swim began very inauspiciously. Just as we were ready to head off to the starting point, Montauk lighthouse, Paul disappeared. He streaked by me on his way to the car, muttering something about needing more throat lozenges. Apparently, as he leaned over the boat while loading it, the lozenges had fallen from his shirt pocket into the water. He returned in a cloud of dust and we leapt onto the boat. Needless to say, throughout that long day I never once coughed. Obviously, my mother is right yet again—saltwater *is* a miraculous cure-all. I didn't actually gargle with it, but the effect appears to have been the same.

Paul and I hadn't done our homework and found ourselves totally unprepared for the problems ahead. It was a rough ride to the lighthouse beach, making Paul seasick from the moment we emerged from the stillness of the harbor. We were behind schedule when we arrived at the start, having wasted too much time lightheartedly making movies. Three boats made up our tiny flotilla: a forty-foot Hatteras, a small motorboat, and an inflatable Zodiac. Tim the navigator, Mark the cameraman, and I tried to go ashore in the Zodiac so that I could start officially from land. It was a nasty pebble beach and the surf hammered us into the rocks, only to grab us maliciously away again and again. Mark was up to his knees in the water, with jeans on, and his feet were bloody. Tim was out there as well, while I held on in the boat as best I could, trying not to think how nauseated I was, feeling silly as I knelt in the rubber raft, clutching the sides, as the two men tried futilely to tow me ashore.

A state-park employee drove up in a pickup truck as we struggled to land the boat and furiously berated us when we explained what we were doing. He thundered on about permits, not the Coast Guard permits we had, but state permits from Albany. He threatened to stop us if we tried to start from his beach. We were already quite late and not in a mood to argue, so we changed tactics. Tim and Mark tried to get the Zodiac out far enough to start the engine, but this time the waves wouldn't let us go, flinging us back toward shore. Why our project would be such a source of anger to someone was totally beyond my comprehension. I forged into the water and towed the Zodiac out to the motorboat, which waited patiently, bobbing just beyond where the waves were breaking. I dragged myself awkwardly into the heaving motorboat and dried off. Paul pulled himself together and greased me up while I hung on for dear life, still managing to slime Paul with lanolin every time I slammed into him. I was ready to quit right then and there, hoping that the park worker would indeed arrest us and take us in. Instead, I pulled on my cap and goggles, yelled, "Honey!" and stole a quick kiss, and jumped into the sea.

The first half hour was enough to make me seriously question my choice of hobbies, if not my sanity. I was seasick, struggling to keep my long-ago breakfast down. The waves tossed me about like the flotsam I was, and this time it wasn't fun. Swarms of jellyfish engulfed me in a translucent cloud of gelatinous bubbles. My new prescription goggles allowed me to see them clearly, instead of as the blurs they had formerly been. One of them brushed against me, then another, then another. Bracing myself for the pain, I awaited the inevitable sting, but it never materialized. They were harmless. Still, I cringed each time I touched one, no matter how often they proved themselves to be benign. Within a short time, my nausea died down. I eased myself into a rhythm: arm over arm, mind over matter. Ella Fitzgerald floated in my mind, enchanting me: "I'm wild again, beguiled again, a simpering, whimpering child again, bewitched, bothered, and bewildered am I." I splashed through waves, rode over the top of them, slid to the bottom, all the while singing and daydreaming and watching Paul, waiting for him to feel better. Repetitive motion frees the mind to wander, but the discipline imposed by the act of swimming keeps one in check. My mind may have been on its way to France, but my stroke count never varied more than two strokes per minute throughout the entire journey.

The first hour is always the longest. It's as if I have to learn time anew. Once that hour has passed, I understand how long it is, that it is not the eternity it seemed before it was over. The difficulty in a swim is not cumulative, does not increase with the amount swum. It ebbs and flows. The chop picks up and settles down. The water is cold, then warm, then something in between. The pain increases somewhere, moves on, then subsides. The only constants are that I am still swimming, and Paul is still seasick. He had laughed at the part in the English Channel manual where they say to make sure that the crew knows to throw up on the far side of the boat. It obviously slipped his mind in the discomfort of the situation, and when I reminded him at a later date, he just laughed again. It didn't really matter where he was; I was acutely aware of his pain. He tried to reassure me, telling me at each feeding that he felt better. Several hours into the swim, someone else on the boat stopped me for food. Concerned, I asked what was wrong with Paul. "I'm okay," he said weakly from the far side of the boat. "Just thought I'd sit this one out."

Not wanting me to worry, he managed to shout, "I love you, li'l Sal" as I pulled my goggles back down over my eyes.

"I love you," I sent back over the waves before starting to swim again.

Paul never seemed to notice hot or cold; his body temperature regulated itself at the same even keel. From early fall through the dead of winter until late spring, he always wore the same battered leather jacket, annoyed when I would ask, "Don't you need a sweater?" or "Aren't you hot?" The afternoon of the Montauk swim I noticed that he progressively wore more and more clothes, shivering as he added my sweats and jacket to his own clothes, until he was wearing every last article of clothing we had brought. Wearing nothing but my thin bathing suit, in water that was not nearly as cool as some I have known, but chilly nonetheless, I feared that Paul was colder than I.

I pulled my way through islands of seaweed, schools of jellyfish, masses of what looked like plant seeds. I asked the people in the boat what they were but they couldn't see them. The surface of water is opaque to those not actually in it, functioning as a scrim does in theatre. When lit from the front, this kind of backdrop is impossible to see through but when lights are focused behind or upstage of it, the fabric becomes translucent. It is used to hide scenes from the audience, to conceal images until the time comes to reveal them. I was the only one who could see these things that surrounded me. It wasn't until dark that the others saw them by shining the light onto the water, breaking the surface. The tiny specks were "sand eels," which makes them sound a lot worse than the innocuous particles they were. Around midday, one of them had found its way ignominiously up my nose, amusing Paul out of his glassy stupor. Treading water, trying to snort the thing out, I was so relieved to see him laugh that it was worth any amount of embarrassment.

The currents weren't doing anything they were supposed to: there was one hour during which I swam four miles; another, only half a mile. The large boat was equipped with loran, allowing distances to be measured. I had smeared grease on my prescription goggles, so I switched back to the normal ones and my world was reduced once more to water, sky, and the blur of a boat. I probably wouldn't have recognized a shark if it was swimming beside me. Paul repeatedly assured me that he could see land just ahead, but like some half-glimpsed truth, it remained out of sight for me. The excitement in his voice sent me flying and I raced over the water. Unfortunately, the tide was against me, and what felt like a sprint was more akin to a dead end.

The sun sank gracefully through the fading sky, shedding glittering teardrops on foam-flecked waves before slipping gravely into the sea at my side. The light drained from above and came to rest in gleaming shards on the mirrored surface of the water, the reflection brighter than the source. We were all entranced by the elegance of that sunset, until the darkness that inescapably followed delivered a new set of problems.

I've done a fair amount of night swimming and the lack of light didn't bother me. "Out of sight is out of mind" did away with the jellyfish threat, finally. The sea had soothed itself into an easy slumber. It was not difficult to see the well-lit boat glowing through the surrounding gloom. However, it was next to impossible for the crew to keep me in sight. They had a light to shine on me, but Paul asked me over and over if I was all right, fearful that he might lose me in that vast emptiness. We had bought clip-on phosphorescent sticks for the Channel swim, but we hadn't thought to bring them along. It wasn't planned that I would swim into the absolute darkness of a starless, moonless night. The clouds had filled the sky as soon as the sun set, obscuring any natural light source.

We stopped for a conference just outside the harbor at Watch Hill. Foolishly, I hadn't switched back to my prescription goggles and was confused by the flickering around me—red buoy lanterns, a fisherman checking his lobster pots, the reflections of lights on shore, as well as the actual lights. The crew told me it was too risky to take the boat beyond the last danger buoy, as there were rocks in the bay. I had the option of swimming to shore alone—and those rocks would still be a problem, but only for me. Walking out of the water is the most satisfying part of a swim, but this time it was not to be. I let Paul make the decision and he read my mind. The swim would officially end when I touched the final danger buoy, some two hundred yards from shore, three minutes short of landfall, nineteen and a half miles from Montauk. I did a final sprint toward the swaying iron mass ahead of me, touched it, and swam back to the cheering boat. Paul pulled me clumsily onto the rear platform. That hug was surely worth the eight hours and fifty-six minutes the swim had taken, more solid than standing on dry land. I was prevented from walking into the water at the start, and chose not to walk out at the finish, but the swim felt complete to me.

The rain started almost as soon as we turned the boats around. Paul and I joined the crew on the large boat, since it had the luxury of a hot shower, which I stood under until it ran cold, washing the sand eels pasted to my body down into the drain. Paul was still wearing my sweats, so the girlfriend of the boat pilot gave me a pair of hers. I drank a can of soda, then joined Paul, who was hanging on to the lurching railing, so I could throw up over the side. Seasickness was not a problem while I was in the water, only when I was floundering above it.

It poured all night and into the day. We drove back the next morning, too exhausted to stick to our original schedule, which had been to return to the city right after the swim. My recovery time was a lot faster than Paul's. I navigated the Long Island Expressway while he tried to convince himself that the swaying of the car was nothing like the rolling of a boat. He called in sick that day and we spent a long, lazy weekend scoffing at how easy the English Channel was going to be. When I went to workout on Saturday, everyone asked about the Montauk swim. It was a bit of a surprise for most people, some of whom only found out about it by reading the newspaper. I had told only my closest friends. If I didn't make it, I didn't want anyone to know. Paradoxically, everyone knew about the English Channel. At first I thought that if everyone knew, I couldn't change my mind, until I realized that was no longer an issue. By then, I was certain I could do it, and it loomed so large in my life it seemed silly to keep it a secret.

We talked of finding someone else to come to England with us. Paul was concerned about being useless because of his sea-sickness. We could think of only one close friend we would want to come along, a long-distance cyclist and runner who had traded off support duties with me over the years, someone whose company we both would enjoy. I understood when Betsy laughed and turned us down, for she liked England less than we, and already had her vacation planned for the same period of time, but I couldn't help feeling a little hurt all the same.

"You're the only one that really loves me," I said, pouting as I hung up the phone. And Paul smiled, content to be my only love, to know the full extent of my dependence on him. We decided to send him to my doctor to get a prescription for the ear patch that people recommended, and let it go at that. There was no one else with whom we wanted to share such special time, no one whose company wouldn't be an intrusion.

AUGUST 1, 1990

It was exactly one week before I was due to leave for England and I was bouncing off the walls, having received word that Ben and Jerry were going to sponsor me for the cost of the boat from England to France, our major expense at that point. It was a well-kept secret, or maybe more of a joke, that I was the official long-distance swimmer of Ben and Jerry's ice cream. We had lost touch over the years, but they were ready to provide generous support once again. Paul's frequent-flier miles were buying my airplane ticket; he was planning to turn the trip into business after the swim, so his passage was covered. All in all, we were doing pretty well at keeping expenses down. Maybe we would even have enough money and time for a weekend in Paris when it was over. Unfortunately, because of immigration bureaucracy, the powers that be require that any swimmer return to England directly upon reaching France. We would have chosen to bring our luggage and passports along, so we could check into a romantic hotel with a hot shower, warm croissants, and the obligatory bottle of champagne.

Swimming the English Channel had become something of a business. The water was generally warmest in August, so that was when most people made the attempt. Because of an accident involving a party boat on the Thames some years before, restrictions were tightened on all boats, including those accompanying Channel swimmers. This meant that there were very few pilots who were licensed and available. Most people plan to swim the Channel at least a year in advance and book their boats accordingly. Our decision was not made until May, leaving us at a disadvantage. We were tentatively scheduled with a pilot but he had several swimmers ahead of me. The best he could promise was, "If the weather holds, everyone can go. If it doesn't, there's the chance that no one will go. So just come over and we'll see what we can do." And if a storm blows up or a heavy fog rolls in at any point, the swim may have to be aborted in the middle, or an hour from France, and one loses one's place in line, as well as one's money. It was difficult to believe that all that work, all that training, hinged on a gamble, that I might not even have the opportunity to swim. But we knew that when we committed ourselves.

The English Channel is part of a tidal stream that originates in the Atlantic Ocean, splitting as part of it flows north between Ireland and Scotland and then south again along the east coast of England, while the rest surges up and down the Dover Strait. The meeting place of the two streams varies with wind and air pressure, which in turn affect the duration and strength of the tidal streams. Spring tides and neap tides further complicate the situation. The latter are tamer but the former are possible, if less preferable. Spring tides occur every two weeks, during the new moon and the full moon. The amount of water moving up and down the Channel is far greater at these times than during the neap tides, which occur several days after the first and last quarters of the moon. All this affects a swimmer because it makes it impossible to traverse the Channel in a straight line, to limit the crossing to the shortest distance between Dover and Cap Gris Nez. Instead, one follows a zigzag or S-shaped path as one is pulled up and down the Channel with the tide, so that the distance covered is much more than the twenty-two miles shown on the map. Swimmers must work with the tides. Starting times are based on slack water and tidal flow and on each individual's speed. It is an inexact science. There are swimmers who have made it to within a mile of France, only to find that they are too late and cannot beat the current, which has turned against them. Strong currents can be impossible to fight, more powerful than any swimmer. The best, and sometimes the only, way to reach land on the other side of a crosscurrent is obliquely, not head-on. The problem with taking this tack to arrive in France is that, because of the geography, one risks being swept down the coast, and running out of land.

We were amused by the information we received from England, by quaint expressions such as the reference to whitecaps as "white horses," or bathing suits as "swimming costumes," by a certain prissiness and a tendency to state the obvious. It all fit in perfectly with our image of swimming the English Channel as a feat with the weight of tradition and time-honored eccentricity behind it. There were quirky rules covering all possibilities. For instance, if one finishes against steep cliffs instead of on a beach, the swim is considered completed when one touches rock, with no seawater beyond. The tone of the handbook was chastising, as if the committee was tired of the kind of people who would decide to swim the Channel without informing the association of heart problems or serious medical conditions, or those who thought it was an easy jaunt that anyone could do, without adequate training. There was a certain annoying smugness in the warning that many swimmers had "travelled across the world to make their attempt on the Channel, and have had to return without even getting their feet wet!"

I suppose that some of the warnings were meant to frighten, but we refused to be intimidated by the requirement that crew members be proficient in first aid and hypothermia resuscitation, or that "a harness or some other lifting device suitable for the vessel in the prevailing conditions must be provided to recover a distressed or unconscious swimmer from the water." This far into our quest, I was absolutely convinced that no one would need to drag me out before I was finished. Gale-force winds or storms might have sent me back to the boat, but I would know, in such a situation, that when they called me in, it was beyond my control and time to stop.

FRIDAY, AUGUST 3, 1990

Paul left work early and we drove up to Paradox one last time. Usually, we went only if we had at least three days, because it was a long drive, but I felt that I needed to touch base, to replenish my spirit before setting sail for England. It turned out to be the most carefree weekend of the summer. My training buddy, Brian, and his girlfriend, Cheryl, were in the area and we swam the lakes, but not seriously, just nice stretch-out jaunts. One morning, while Paul and Cheryl were relaxing in lawn chairs on the beach, Brian and I swam off, intending to do my habitual three-mile swim. Instead, as soon as we lost sight of land, we stopped to tread water, and chatted until it was time to swim back. For some reason, the pressure was off. The difficult part was over, it was okay to enjoy ourselves until the final test. Paul finally went for a swim, the first time that year that the water was warm enough for him. We had a party for Brian, and for me. Friends and neighbors sat around the eight-foot-long kitchen table laughing, talking, and eating brownies with ice cream and hot fudge and whipped cream.

I had thought that gaining weight would be the fun part of preparing for the Channel, but it turned out to be something of an ordeal. I have all the normal weight neuroses of a modern woman, so deep down inside I didn't really want to be fat. And it wasn't that easy to schedule meals between swims so that I would have the food I wanted when I wanted it. I spent too much time swimming and traveling between watering holes to worry about calories. But I had managed to gain about ten pounds, which is a lot when one is not very tall. Fat is the best natural insulation. It does not conduct heat well, so it serves as a blanket, keeping the body warm in the constant battle against the greedy cold water.

Marathon-swimming rules stipulate that one is allowed to wear one suit, one cap, a pair of goggles, and nothing more. Grease is permitted, but it wears off throughout the course of the swim. Paul read the rules carefully, trying to find a way to give me an edge, to make it easier, to help me stay warm. He suggested attaching feathers to my suit, not as Icarus did, but in imitation of a duck, to repel water and help retain heat. I assured him that not only would it be illegal; I would refuse to wear such a thing.

At a certain point in our relationship, Paul watched someone cut my hair to its standard short, tousled length, and decided that he could do it just as well. I was still too much of a tomboy to feel comfortable in a beauty parlor, so I was more than willing to let him. Instead of self-conscious ordeals, haircuts became sensually playful treats. He laughed when I wondered how the professionals managed to cut my bangs without sitting in my lap, said they obviously didn't know what they were doing. He stopped cutting my hair in May, figuring that even an extra inch under my cap would add a little warmth, regretful that we hadn't thought of it earlier.

S U N D A Y ,   A U G U S T   5 ,   1 9 9 0

We went to one of those popular swimming holes which would have gone unnoticed by the casual passerby but for all the cars lining the side of the road. A waterfall spills over a cliff, splashing into a deep pool. I held my breath as Paul leapt into the void, exhaling only when he came up to the surface for air. Over and over I watched, my heart in my mouth, as he laughed and shivered and leapt. His skin was translucent in the greenish light glowing through the trees, his eyes thrilled with boyish wonder. He urged me to try it but I timidly refused, unwilling to trust my skill at jumping just the right distance, unable to trust that I would be caught by the familiar water instead of the unforgiving rock.

I didn't think I had swum enough that day, so we went to Chapel Pond. It lies at the bottom of a gorge, alongside the road to Lake Placid, with sheer rock walls soaring above it. It always made me a little breathless to swim there, something about the massive cliffs looming over the dark teal water. Paul paddled around while I swam. Treading water in the center, we heard voices riccochet high above. Confused by the echoes, we didn't see them right away, the tiny spots of color scattered among the rocks. I imagined the climbers clinging to some imperceptible crevasse, and wondered how on earth they could do that. My chosen sport seemed so staid and boring compared to hanging off a mountainside. The thrill of overcoming wind and waves and long distances was enough for me. I had asked Paul if it was boring in the boat beside me, whether he grew tired of seeing nothing but water and me swimming. He assured me that it wasn't, that between feedings, and stroke counts, and taking the temperature, there was too much to do. And the times when it was just me in the water with him rowing at my side, it was peaceful and pleasant, and not the least bit boring. Paul would sometimes stand in the canoe, to stretch, he said, oblivious to my warnings. The boat never even came close to tipping, but I was convinced he stood to tempt fate, to add a hint of danger to the monotony.

That afternoon Paul carried in load after load of firewood, ignoring me as I lazily teased him. "Are you making sure there's enough wood for the whole winter? It's only the beginning of August. We'll be back before it gets cold."

We left even more regretfully than usual that Sunday evening. Stopping to visit at Lottie's house on our way out of town, we sat on the dock; we were never far from water that summer. I remember saying, "Pretty soon, when we live in Saratoga or Burlington, we won't have to drive back down on Sunday nights." We had decided that these were places we could agree on, fulfilling our different criteria of "livable cities." I knew I didn't want to be a scenic artist forever; five-gallon buckets of paint, horrible locations, and the "business" were wearing me down.

Paul couldn't make up his mind between opening a hardware/paint/turtle store, starting a tool-rental business, or applying himself to another of his many book ideas—to add to the two already published. Mostly he wanted to live in a small town. He was fed up with New York, with the noise and the dirt, with the nonstop low-level fear. I think he would have been long gone from the city if he hadn't met me, and sometimes I almost felt sorry for him, for falling for me, and having his life change course from the one he had planned. He assumed he would end up teaching college in some idyllic town, wearing those silly cardigans with the leather patches on the elbows, playing with our grandchildren.

Moving to New York felt like coming home to me, a place where I could disappear, not feel odd, knowing that there was always someone odder just down the block. "Fitting in" was not an issue. Sometimes I felt like a fraud, pretending to dislike New York. I had my moments, of course, such as going out to the car one day to drive to work and finding it gone, or being done in by the oppressive summer heat and the accompanying stench. But still I sensed that anything was possible there; that walking down the street, one was sure to see something interesting, that we could decide totally spontaneously to see a play and five minutes later would be on our way to an unforgettable evening in the theatre. I never had any desire to be surrounded by people exactly like myself, who thought as I did, whose backgrounds were the same as mine. Such a situation did not strike me as comfortable, but rather limiting.

The people we knew in New York came from all over the world, and fascinated me with the diversity of their lives, and the stories they could tell. There is a European quality to the city, a sensibility far from that of suburbia which I had found so stifling. One characteristic is a certain warmth between friends. Paul, who was by nature more subdued than I, found the effusive physicality too much. He was annoyed that he was expected to kiss friends hello; it did not come naturally to him. So he finally refused, telling me that he didn't want to waste his kisses on people who didn't matter to him, that he would rather save them all for me. As if he knew he had only a finite amount.

Gregg took publicity pictures for Ben and Jerry, just for fun, photos of me sitting on a deck chair with Paradox Lake shimmering at my back as I pretended to eat ice cream from a pint container. It was pretense because we had eaten all the ice cream at our little party and the container was completely empty. There were pictures of Paul as well, which turned out far better than those of me. It was late by the time we tore ourselves away from the tranquillity of that evening and entered the endless stream of cars flooding back into New York.

TUESDAY, AUGUST 7, 1990

After morning workout I spent the day trudging the sweltering streets of Manhattan, trying to make headway in the list of last-minute chores and purchases, leaving too many things for Paul to do. I was flying to England the next evening, but Paul wasn't following until Friday night. We had decided that I needed more time to acclimate and we didn't want to squander any of his vacation days, in case we had to wait out foul weather in the Channel. My feet were aching by the time I appeared at Paul's office in the late afternoon, hot and dusty, laden with shopping bags. I showed him my purchases, including a gift I had bought for myself. I was a little ashamed that I had spent money on something frivolous, but he smiled when he saw it, and declared it worth the money. It was a T-shirt with a bevy of turtles on the front, drawn with shells in crazy patterns. In the middle of the shirt was scrawled, "Why be normal?"

Paul was so proud of me, leading me around the office so everyone could wish me luck. He talked me out of my weariness, into eating out for a send-off dinner. I knew that he had ulterior motives, that he coveted the leftover Chinese food in the fridge for the next night when he would be home alone, so I willingly went along for a last supper at his favorite Italian restaurant, a place named Fiasco. There was one particular dish which we both liked best; he insisted I order it, I let him finish what I couldn't eat. I sipped his red wine. I was trying not to drink, to be as strong and healthy as I could be.

We talked of things I no longer remember, except for one. I recounted an incident that had happened that day when I was crossing Sixth Avenue to pick up the proofs of the pictures taken in Paradox. A taxi was turning onto the avenue, trying to cut me off, even though, as a pedestrian in a designated crosswalk with the "walk" sign lit, I had the right of way. I made eye contact with the driver, glared at him as I continued walking, forcing him to yield. It seemed such a victory at the time.

That night, holding each other in the summer darkness, the

fan at the end of the bed gently whirring, sending a soft breeze our way, we regretted that we weren't traveling together, wondered how we were going to survive two days and two nights apart. Paul fretted that I might have the opportunity to swim the Channel before he got there, a totally impossible scenario. I promised I wouldn't—not a difficult promise, because I knew I could never make it without him. "But what if, the day you arrive, they say you can go now—the conditions are perfect, but you have to leave right away?"

"Don't worry," I hushed him. "It won't happen. I'll wait for you." He smiled, smug in the assurance of his place in the venture, in my life.

W E D N E S D A Y ,   A U G U S T   8 ,   1 9 9 0

We had decided that I had a better chance of sleeping on the plane if I went to workout as usual. So that last morning I drowsily tore myself out of bed, out of Paul's arms, at about 5:40, having stolen a few extra minutes from the alarm clock. He wanted me to stay but I didn't want to be late for my last workout. He walked me to the door and stood there, sweetly, gently, achingly beautiful. It seems to me that we hugged and fussed more than usual, I already, eternally, regretting that I had decided to leave. I couldn't keep my hands from the smooth coolness of his skin. He was naked the last time I saw him alive, young and lean and strong. "I'm going to need a lot of phone calls today, honey." He smiled resignedly. "I love you so much"—my voice muffled in his chest, my head pressed against his heart.

"And I love you, li'l Sal."

I heard the door click shut behind me, drove off to the pool, and swam the workout. Everyone wished me luck. One woman, who had swum the Channel, told me how the French lifeguard barely let her rest on the beach, insisting that she go back to her boat, seemingly worried that she was trying to sneak into the country. And when she arrived back in England, the woman in charge informed her rather coldly that her swim wouldn't be official until all the paperwork was finished. Brian gave me a blue plastic good-luck dolphin wrapped in a note which said, "Hey Sally—Thanks so much and good luck to you and Paul. I will always be on the side opposite the boat, pushing you." I thought my life was wonderful. I didn't know that by then it was over.

I went home to pack. I was so wound up and excited that I could barely get anything done. I waited for Paul to phone, but when I couldn't figure out how to set up the tape player to copy a CD, I called him, only to be told that he hadn't arrived. I was confused, sure that he would have been there by then, since he was gone by the time I got home. In my misguided egotism I thought, maybe he's somewhere buying me a surprise for a send-off present. I left a message for him to call me and went about my chores. Paul had made a list on the computer of everything to bring, to be done. It seemed that I just added to it, instead of crossing things off. I left the lanolin for him to pack, to reassure him that I meant it when I said I wouldn't swim without him. I left too many things for him, hoping he wouldn't be annoyed that his suitcase would be filled with my things, knowing that it would be fine. I packed the same hot-pink suit I had worn in the Montauk swim. I knew Paul would bring his good-luck shirt, the one he wore on Lake George and on Long Island Sound. He didn't mind that it was covered with grease stains from the lanolin any more than I minded that my suit was still caked with the stuff.

I went to the basement to put laundry in the washing machines. I was sure the message light would be flashing on the answering machine when I returned, but it wasn't. The worry was starting to weigh on me. But still I had no premonition. It was, after all, a bright, sunny summer morning. How could the arrival of the police come as such a shock? In novels and movies, the characters always know. They feel a cold breeze, or hear a cry, or sense disaster.

The buzzer rang. I asked who it was into the intercom. "Police," they said. And in that instant, the Moment began, when time became unrecognizable to me, when I commenced the struggle to stop it from moving forward. I opened the door, my hand already trembling. The apartment was one flight up, but people always thought it was on the ground floor and had difficulty finding it. I stood in the hallway to tell the police to come up the stairs. There were two officers, both men, neither of whom wanted to be there any more than I. "How are you related to Paul Carter?" the first one asked, reading the name from a slip of paper as the second one kept an uneasy distance.

The Moment, if time itself can have emotional components, took on an element of terror, and persisted in progressing.

"I am his wife," I replied, my voice coming from a great distance, sounding to me like a record being played at the wrong speed, and at the wrong volume. I instantly regretted having spoken, for that allowed the Moment to lunge ahead, to escape. My mind and my body separated; those things that one does unconsciously to survive, I did, but in an unnatural way. I forgot to breathe, or maybe I hyperventilated, but either way, the act of taking in oxygen was out of kilter, or maybe it was that the oxygen was not going where it should. Anything that happened on a physical level was a betrayal of what was happening mentally, infusing reality with a disjointed quality. I knew that I couldn't bear to hear what I sensed could come next, but try as I might, I couldn't keep it from coming. Or maybe I was too stunned to put all I had into it; if I hadn't been thrown off-balance, I could have fought back harder, stood my ground, dug in my heels, stopped time. But like a wave at Jones Beach, the force of it knocked me over, and swept me away before I had caught my breath, before I was ready. I no longer had a say in what happened to me or mine.

The police stepped into the apartment. Well, one did; the other one wouldn't cross the threshold, so the door stayed open. The first one forged ahead, anxious to be done with this moment, oblivious to all I was doing to hold it back. He wouldn't look at me, unwilling to see what his words were doing, just wanting this to be over, to move on to the rest of his day. He told me that Paul had been in an accident, that he was in St. Vincent's Hospital, that I should call a Dr. Burns: Here, write down this number. It must be all right, after all, he gave the police our address, that's what I thought. They wouldn't tell me how he was, said they didn't know, just that I should call the number, not to worry yet.

I started talking, rapidly, to slow things down, reassuring them that we had witnessed a similar incident the year before and that it had turned out okay. We had been walking toward Fifth Avenue one bright, sunny Saturday afternoon. Standing on the street corner, we debated whether we should head downtown to a certain store to buy a birthday present for my best friend from high school, or head east to browse in a large home-design store. Leslie's gift won, so we had started walking downtown, instead of crossing the avenue, when we heard the unmistakable, unforgettable shriek of brakes. Turning, looking back to where we had been standing instants before, we saw a taxi jump the curb with a woman, a pedestrian who had been in the crosswalk, somehow on its hood. The cab crashed into the building, throwing the woman against the brick wall, then to the pavement. I gasped for air as I stood frozen, tears streaming. Paul gently turned me around, said, "Don't look," and rushed over to the woman. I looked frantically for a phone, saw a doorman, screamed, "Call 911!" as if he hadn't already done so, then stood helplessly, amid others who were also paralyzed, unable to lift our feet from the sidewalk. Paul was still by her side when the ambulance arrived, stayed there as the paramedics worked. Come back here, I thought, trying to communicate with Paul telepathically. You can't do any more for her. You'll just be in the way. And, finally, as they put her in the ambulance, he jogged over to me.

"Is she alive? Did you talk to her?"

"Yes, yes. She's okay. She can move her feet and her hands. She's conscious"—his arms around me for reassurance. "She wants me to go to the hospital with her."

"So go," I said, pushing him away, generous in my relief. "Don't worry about me."

"Are you sure?"

"Absolutely." I knew that one of Paul's greatest fears was that something would happen to him on the streets of New York, surrounded by strangers, alone.

"I'll meet you at the pool in a few hours." We had planned to swim that afternoon. I watched the ambulance drive away. Unwilling to lose it, at a loss, I followed it the few blocks to St. Vincent's Hospital. I was standing out front, trying to figure out what to do, trying to overcome my hatred of hospitals, when Paul walked out the door. He wasn't allowed to stay with her any longer. He had called her husband; he was on his way. We visited her in the hospital the next day, brought her flowers. Her back was broken, but she recovered. We had dinner at their apartment once. I didn't return their Christmas card the following year. I thought it better to be considered rude than for her to find out what had happened. It was several years later, when her case was coming to trial, that her lawyer tried to call Paul at work and was told. She called me, couldn't believe what she had heard. By then they had a child. She left it up to me, call if you want to get together, but I never did.

I babbled a shorter version of that story at the police as they tried to escape, to show them it would be okay. When they were gone, I called Dr. Burns. I thought I was being reasonable and composed while the officers were there, but I still have the scrap of paper on which I had carefully written the doctor's name. It is barely legible, scrawled shakily, the way a child would write, or a woman who had lost everything. Dr. Burns was calm and very gentle. Paul was in surgery. Alive! I thought, not knowing then the deceptions of modern medicine. "Do you have a way to get to the hospital?" he asked.

"I have a car."

"No. Don't drive. Just get a cab and come down here. Try to call a friend or relative to meet you here." I called my friend Mary, who worked in midtown. She said she was on her way. I rushed down to the basement, took my clothes out of the washing machine, dumped them on the floor in the middle of the foyer, wondering as I did so how I could be so practical at such a time, who cared about the laundry for heaven's sake, but maybe it was just another futile attempt to make things stay as they were, to make believe nothing had happened. I was a normal person emptying a washing machine, except that the clothes were wet and soapy, and I was shaking so badly I could barely hold on to the sopping fabric, and my shallow breaths made strange whimpering sounds. I changed my shirt because I knew it was one Paul didn't like, and put on a T-shirt we had bought in Hawaii, covered with fluorescent fish, to cheer him up. I shoved my engagement ring onto the finger with my wedding band. I didn't wear it every day because it was delicate filigree, old, but I was trying for anything that could be lucky. I even grabbed a book to read, to have something to do at his bedside, until he woke up.

Running down the street, I searched frantically for a cab, jumped into the first one I saw. The driver didn't speak English; instead of shouting the name of the hospital as I slammed the door, I should have given the street address. He drove the wrong way as we neared the highway, mistaking Columbia Presbyterian for St. Vincent's, brakes screeching as he made the turn at the last minute. I screamed directions at him, as we sped from one traffic jam to another. All the traffic lights were conspiring against me.

What happened was this. Paul was walking across Eighth Avenue at Twenty-fifth Street on his way to work when a twenty-year-old hotshot behind the wheel of a truck decided that a light that had barely turned red wasn't going to stop him. It took the ambulance twenty minutes to reach Paul, even though he was only ten blocks from the hospital. I was told later that the police found me through the doctor's phone number on the prescription for seasick medication that was in his pocket.

Throwing money at the cabdriver, I leapt from the car as it pulled to a stop, awkward in my brittle movements. I fought my way through the heaviness of the stagnant heat only to run into a wall of ice-cold, antiseptic-reeking hospital air. Mary was already there. As we waited, not knowing how bad it was, I actually worried about making my flight, thought how chagrined Paul would be when he realized he had made me miss it, decided that it wouldn't be so bad because now we would just fly to England together. Broken arm, I was praying, or broken leg. It would be clumsy on the boat, his leg in a cast, but insignificant, a reminder of what we almost lost.

Dr. Burns, a truly kind and compassionate man, put us in a room away from the main waiting area and said that the surgeon would be right in, then knelt at my side, trying to hold me, as the stranger in green fatigues delivered the blow. He droned on and on, refusing to let my sobs silence him, or sway him from what needed to be said. He told me they wouldn't know for sure until after the operation that was still being performed, but the prognosis was grim. Both of Paul's wrists were broken, but they weren't going to set them unless it was necessary, as if I couldn't figure out what that meant. The brain suffers irreversible damage after four to six minutes without oxygen; he'd not breathed for twenty minutes, an eternity.

One night, while Paul and I were sitting in bed, side by side, reading, one of us noticed an ad for a contest. It was a promotion for a movie that was about to be released. There was to be a competition, in a tank filled with water in Times Square, for the couple who could kiss underwater for the longest period of time. The record was about three and a half minutes, if memory serves. So Paul and I took turns timing each other holding our breath. I was sure I would win, but he did, lasting excruciatingly close to the record. It was such a long time, those interminable minutes of aching, burning concentration. We didn't actually enter the contest—we couldn't figure out how we could last longer than a couple seconds, lips pressed together, underwater, without laughing away all our precious oxygen.

The surgeon persisted in going on, using French words, Latin words, English that sounded familiar but made no sense, explaining relentlessly. But he had left the neurosurgeon with Paul, so maybe . . . I wouldn't know more until the operation was finished. Someone told us where to wait, then lost track of us.

I called Paul's sister in Colorado, told her I was sure he would pull through, surely she knew how stubborn he could be, but she wanted to make plane reservations and assured me she would tell their father as best she could. Mary called my sister, left it to her to find our parents. I relied on others to weave the tapestry of tragedy. We waited, and waited, and waited. Friends stopped by, people from Paul's office, then left. The sterile, impersonal waiting room looked out onto the street. I couldn't bear to see people going about their normal lives, so I sat with my back to the windows, watching for Paul to walk in, convinced that he had been mugged, his wallet stolen, that it was a case of mistaken identity, that it was a stranger in the operating room, someone I hadn't just kissed goodbye, a person who meant nothing to me.

The next surgeon was as bad as the first. How do people learn to be so cold and impersonal in the face of unspeakable tragedy? Is it a class taught in medical school? It apparently comes with age and experience; the residents were kind, as were the nurses. Maybe they could see themselves in me, feared it could happen to them, knew that compassion was the most they could offer. This surgeon stated that he had been looking everywhere for us. Paul was out of surgery, on his way to the ICU. They would keep him on life support for twenty-four hours. If there was no sign of brain activity by then, and he said there wouldn't be, that would be it. He told me that if Paul were to live, he wouldn't be anyone I knew, and I wouldn't want him to exist like that. As if he knew what I wanted, as if I wouldn't give anything to have Paul alive in any condition.

They told me what floor to go to. Somehow, as I waited for the elevator, the policeman who had been at the accident scene appeared. He introduced himself and said he was there to visit his brother, who was in rehab after a similar accident. His brother had been with a friend when they were crossing the street, and the friend had died, but his brother was about to be released from the hospital, and that was the only part of the story I could hear. That and his sympathy, his concern in seeking me out. The small kindnesses shone through the haze of misery.

Two nurses led me to Paul, one on either side, ready to catch me, to lend support. They warned me about how he looked. I knew that this was the last chance for error, the last chance for the person I was about to see not to be Paul. Then I could escape from this nightmare and try to find him, so we could have the rest of our lives together, to reminisce about the time that horrible mistake was made.

His head was swathed in bandages, his eyes were black and swollen, there was a breathing tube in his mouth, but it was, unequivocally and irrevocably, Paul. The nurses held on tight, talking to me, telling me what to do. "It's thought that coma victims hear what's being said to them, and that it helps. Talk to him, just keep talking. Maybe he can hear. Go ahead." I had been talking to him all day, in my mind; saying the words aloud seemed strange. I was self-conscious at first, with the nurses standing there listening, but it didn't take longer than a heartbeat to forget everything and everyone except Paul.

So I started talking, talked for all I was worth, tried to find the words that would save my life. I begged, ordered, cajoled Paul to come back to me, to open his swollen eyes, to prove the experts wrong. Paul had always told me how much he loved me; I challenged him to prove it. It's only words unless you act on them, I reminded him. I promised him anything he wanted, used every incentive I could think of, talked until words lost their meaning. And on and on through that endless afternoon and night and morning, endless except that I didn't want it to end because I was afraid of the outcome, afraid that Paul wasn't really listening, that he was already gone. Each minute was an eternity, every hour too quickly past. I wouldn't let him rest, refused to be ignored, please don't leave me, don't you dare leave me, changed my tone to find one that would work, one that would reach him. I could see that he wasn't breathing on his own when they took the oxygen tube out periodically to clean it. Breathe, Paul, come on, just breathe. But his chest wouldn't rise, all was still, until they replaced the tube and the pretense of life was restored. His body temperature had fallen dangerously low. It was my turn to search under the heating blankets for his icy hand, to hold it in mine, which was equally cold, to remind him of those times I had warmed to his touch and arrived safely home. Surely he could do the same for me. The nurse told me that I didn't have to be so strong, that I didn't have to try so hard, but I knew otherwise. If I asked Paul to do the impossible, I had to be willing to do the impossible for him. That was how we lived.

I have never been as cold in my life as I was that night. A friend of Paul's brought me a heavy pullover, but it didn't matter. No amount of clothing would ever make me warm again. The shivering came from deep inside, from depths that heat couldn't reach. A sweater would barely affect the surface. My tears felt warm; all else was ice.

My parents arrived sometime that evening. I assured them that Paul would be okay, that he was unbelievably stubborn. Shortly before, a jogger, a woman, had been found beaten in Central Park, had lost vast amounts of blood, hadn't been expected to live. But she did, and surely, I reasoned, if she could, Paul could; if the doctors had been wrong then, they could be wrong now. They weren't the gods they thought they were, deciding who would live and who would not. Surely this couldn't

107

be the end, even seeing what I saw, hearing what I was told; there was too much left unsaid, too much left unlived. I sent my parents off to their hotel, said they should try to sleep. There was nothing they could do at the hospital; I was taking care of everything.

Sometime during the night there was a phone call. The nurse came over to me looking puzzled and told me a man who said he was Paul's cousin was on the line. Confused by a sudden fear of all I didn't know about Paul, I searched through my memories of his family, unable to remember any cousins, except the distant ones in England. I picked up the phone. It was dead. The nurse told me she thought it was the man who killed Paul, because of the way he asked about Paul's condition, how he made up the family connection when she told him she could give information only to family members. She had told the stranger that Paul was in extremely critical condition. It was a shock for me to hear the words, so convinced was I that he would pull through. Shivering, I walked back to Paul's cubicle, sat in the chair, rested my forehead on the bed.

Toward dawn, or what the clock on the wall indicated was dawn, Paul's arm jerked. I was jolted out of my chair, ran next door to the nurse, shouting, "He moved his arm! He moved!" She followed me back into his room, warning me that it was probably nothing more than an involuntary muscle tremor, that it probably didn't mean anything. But it gave me hope. I ignored her experience, her knowledge, and focused on the change, on the fact that for the first time in all that day, and all that night, Paul had moved. How could that not mean anything?

A few hours, or a few minutes later, something else happened, something I knew was bad. Buzzers and lights started going off. Nurses and doctors rushed in, asked me to please leave. I paced up and down the corridor, my arms held tight across my chest, as if I could keep my heart from shattering, as if I could physically hold myself together. I sensed that they were no longer keeping Paul alive for me, but for other reasons. There was a pay phone in the hallway. I thought about calling a good friend who I knew was up at dawn every day, but then I thought how horrible it would be for her to make it through a day at work knowing what she would know. I couldn't be so cruel.

I wasn't back in the room for very long when the surgical entourage entered, asked me to leave once more. This was it, I knew, and I silently pleaded, please Paul, or God, or anyone, I'll never ask for anything else as long as I live, I'll do anything, give anything, my own life, which is worthless anyway without him, whatever it takes, just let this man live.

I didn't realize until months later that when they told me it was time to say goodbye to him, the death certificate had already been signed. He looked no different. What had changed between life and death? They had called me into the waiting room to join my parents. The nurse who had been on duty all night, her shift finished, stayed on, sat with us, offered anything she could do to help. My father sobbed, loud, hoarse, frightening noises, and slumped over on the sofa. My mother wept silently, tears streaming down her contorted face, reaching out to hold me, but I would not be held. I wailed, the only words I could think of, the words that spun around in my mind over and over, "I love him so much," sank into myself, crying, choking, until I raced into the bathroom, falling to my knees on the tile floor.

There was a stranger in the waiting room. I could tell that this was an uncomfortable moment for him, but that infinitesimal part of me that was still sane was expecting it. The question was organ donation. It was left to me to decide, and all I could do was make what to me was the only choice. To have the opportunity to enable someone else to live could be the only good to come out of the situation. As muddled and distraught as I was, I knew this one thing to be true. My hand signed the forms, in a signature that looked remarkably like mine. If it had really been me signing, the pen would have snapped in two, the ink would have sprayed over the neatly typed pages.

I was left alone with Paul. I wept my farewell, tried to wrap my arms around him without disturbing the tubes. When he was in a silly mood, and had done something stupid, he would put his arm over my shoulders, lean on me, and say, "We're as one, li'l Sal. That's what they said in the marriage ceremony." So I assured him that we were still one and that I would live for him and that I loved him so much that if one of us had to go through this, I would rather it be me, that surely he was the lucky one, to be oblivious, to feel nothing. I was being noble, and foolish. But I was certain that between death and being left behind, the latter had to be worse.

That evening, after everyone finally left me alone in our apartment, I frantically looked for him. I searched his pockets, his dresser drawers, called up folders I had never seen on the computer. I played the tape on the answering machine to hear his voice, but a friend had come during the night to gather some things for me and had inadvertently erased all the messages. I found a fossilized bagel in the pocket of a suit he hadn't worn for at least three years, because I didn't like it. I found a present he had bought months before but had apparently forgotten to give me. I buried my face in the sleeves of his shirts hanging in the bedroom closet, sobbed into the fabric, astonished that I wasn't running out of tears, not knowing then that I had an infinite amount. I steeped myself, lost myself in him, absorbed all I could while I could still smell his scent on the pillowcases. I drugged myself with his presence until the sleeping pill sheltered me from his absence.

AUGUST 10, 1990

My mother showed up at our apartment in the early morning. She had been distressed that I wouldn't let her stay the night with me. I had already started to drift away from those I loved, to find it unbearable to be among people. After I let her in, I retreated into silence, lying on the worn white coverlet that Paul's parents had bought at a garage sale and that we had taken when Paul's father sold their house after his wife died. The blinds were drawn in our bedroom, the door closed. It was cool and dark. My eyes were swollen, burning. I cried or I stared into space or I closed my eyes. I was on my side, curled into as small a space as possible, arms around Paul's soaked pillow, praying to be numb, to not feel anything ever again. There was the almost constant murmur of voices from the living room, the muffled ring of the telephone as relatives and friends called with flight information and questions.

Paul's sister and brother-in-law had arrived late the afternoon before. They had driven straight to the hospital, and had seen Paul, which surprised me, for I thought he would already have been in surgery. When they told me this, I thought maybe there was a mistake, maybe they found a way, maybe they had been too hasty to pronounce him dead. I would easily forgive them for putting me through this, it wouldn't matter, anything to have him back. But there was no phone call from the hospital. I had given my parents my address book, and a list of names. They, with the help of friends, took care of everything, until my mother came in to tell me we had to make funeral arrangements and it would be better if I came along to choose a place.

I pulled on a black cotton sundress. It may have been inappropriate—too casual, sleeveless—but it was black. I had bought it on sale for five dollars for my sister when she was pregnant because it was large and shapeless, a dress one could get lost in. We had taken a family trip to Hawaii, our parents, my sister, her husband, Paul, and myself. I gave the dress to her there. She hated it, so I kept it. There had been a certain amount of tension on that vacation. Paul and I had been fighting, mostly at my instigation, it being my family, after all, so at his urging we went off to another island, Kauai, for two days on our own, two of the best days of my life. We arrived at the airport having arranged to rent the cheapest car available only to see others driving off in Mustang convertibles. Smiling, shrugging, we upgraded, so I could have a chance to be Mustang Sally for a while. We rode off to our hotel, wind in our faces, exhilarated by the speed and the scenery. After staying just long enough to check in and giggle at the giant seashell sink, we spent the next twenty-four hours rushing around the island, trying to experience it all. We drove to the northern edge, toured the coast in an inflatable boat, snorkeled, then hiked along the cliffs. One of our wedding gifts had been a photograph taken by a friend of Paul's from this same path. It fascinated us because it was impossible to see the horizon, to know where the ocean stopped and the sky began. We tried to find the spot, snapping many pictures in an unsuccessful attempt to duplicate the illusion of an endless expanse of brilliant blue.

The next day we drove to a waterfall that I read about in the guidebook. It seemed to be hundreds of feet high, this cascade of tumbling, furious water. A path to the bottom was mentioned in the text. We found it, overgrown, muddy, and mosquito-ridden. The noise at the bottom was deafening, terrifying. I was wearing a bathing suit under my shorts; Paul had assumed he wouldn't want to swim, so he hadn't bothered. The pool was irresistible, so he stripped and swam naked, unconcerned about the tourists far above. No one else found our path. The force of the thundering water was deliciously thrilling. Paul, of course, swam much closer to the point of impact than I did, oblivious, as always, to my laughing warnings.

I wore this black cotton dress that reminded me of Hawaii as we walked out of the apartment building into what must have been heat, blinking against the summer sunshine. My parents stood on either side of me, as they had when they walked me down the aisle at our wedding, but Paul was not waiting for me at the end of the sidewalk, just the cab to take us downtown. Moving slowly, concentrating on putting one foot in front of the other, I felt like a ghost, invisible. I immediately recognized the comfort in wearing black. People were going about their lives in some strange, silent pantomime, while I watched from the wings, unseen. These performers were only acting as if nothing had happened. They must have known that the past few days were impossible, and therefore unreal.

We went to the funeral home recommended by the hospital. I hated the mustard-colored wallpaper and the musty smell. We took a cab to look at another place. As we drove up Eighth Avenue, I screamed in my head, "No, no! Please don't go this way! I can't bear to see the corner." But I couldn't say the words. I clenched my teeth as we passed Twenty-fifth Street, looked straight ahead, forced myself to see nothing, held my breath.

I settled for the third funeral home we visited. The service was planned for Sunday because we were unsure when the coroner would release the body. The efficient woman in charge took care of all the details, and offered to call the newspapers to place the obituary, if we would write it. It was barely a struggle to find the words, not worth the pain to go beyond the standards: died suddenly, beloved husband of, devoted son of, etc.

AUGUST 11, 1990

Paul's ashes arrived in a small, plain aluminum canister, surely not large enough to contain all it held. Even though I spent most of the day alone in our room, I waited until the voices were silent, until the apartment door clicked shut for the last time and I had double-locked it. Sitting on the edge of our bed, the tin resting on my lap, I took a screwdriver to the lid, prying it carefully open. It was a fine gray powder, but not uniformly fine. I sifted through the soft dust, searched for larger pieces, something, anything recognizable, until it all blurred together. Moistened by tears, the ashes slipped through my fingers, leaving imperceptible particles embedded in my skin. I poured some into another container, a secret stash, so that when I buried the rest, I would still have some just for me.

A U G U S T   1 2 ,   1 9 9 0

There was a memorial service in New York. Because we had not been part of any religious organization, I didn't know where to turn for a person to officiate at the funeral. Someone suggested the Universalist minister who had married us less than two and a half years before. To find her number, I searched through the notebook where I had written the results of all our wedding research, blinding myself to all but her name. She came to the apartment the night before the funeral, to talk, to know what to say the next day. It was raining hard, it was late in the evening, I hated making anyone leave their house on such a night. I sensed her discomfort, her sorrow at how precipitately the end had followed the beginning. She had a stern, austere quality which had added solemnity to the wedding, but which was perhaps more appropriate for the funeral.

We sat stiffly, side by side on the sofa. Words stuck in my throat; I choked on sentences. Nothing more than monosyllabic answers had been required of me until then. I had lost the ability to talk, to make sense through speech. But I managed to tell her a story, to try to show her how it had been between us. We used to have this silly, but deeply sincere, thing we did. Randomly, at odd moments, one or the other of us would become suddenly very affectionate, smothering the other with kisses, saying, as explanation, "I just got overwhelmed by love," always drawing out the word "love," as in the country songs Paul teased me about listening to. After the Montauk swim, Paul told me that sometime during that afternoon, somewhere in the middle of Long Island Sound, while he was watching me swim, his eyes filled with tears and he was "overwhelmed by love." I brushed it off, joked that he must have been more seasick than I knew, but he had to know what that meant to me, that while I was so worried about how miserable he felt, so guilt-ridden about what I was putting him through, he was thinking about how much he loved me.

Paul's picture, the one taken at Paradox Lake that last weekend, exactly one week before, was at the front of the chapel. The photograph is black and white. Paul is smiling, laughter wrinkles evident at the corners of his eyes, hair mussed, the lake calm at his side. He is wearing a white cotton polo shirt with narrow navy stripes, the one I will take to France, and sunglasses that we bought in Hawaii hanging from a neck strap on which "Kauai" is printed over and over. I take a flower from one of the arrangements scattered around and lay it in front of the photograph, as if at an altar. I don't know what else to do.

Somehow, after the service, I found myself alone, on the opposite side of the hallway from my family, and Paul's. I wanted to walk over to where they were, or have them come over to my side, but I was unable to move, and they stayed where they were. Friends filed past, crying, awkwardly trying to hug me, not knowing what to say any more than I did. One couple, a friend of Paul's and his wife, we had last seen at their wedding, and we had never received a thank-you note for the gift we mailed off later, a set of copper bowls. "Did you ever get the present we sent?" I asked. Apologetically they said they had, but had been remiss in their acknowledgments. "Oh, don't worry about it. It's just that we always wondered . . ." Another friend wept in my arms, repeating over and over, "You are so precious to me." He had barely known Paul, but he knew. My cousin who sublet my apartment when I moved into Paul's had flown in from Brussels, where he was living then. A friend who had relocated to California came back for the funeral. Paul and I had taken her out to dinner on her twenty-fifth birthday, to a cozy Italian restaurant. My dinner made me sick and I spent most of the night in the bathroom, Paul asking sleepily if there was anything he could do. My best friend from high school was there from Pittsburgh; I had been her maid-of-honor, she had held one of the four poles of our chuppah—ours hadn't been a religious wedding, it was a visual thing. We used an antique lace bedspread through which my scenic-artist friends had woven flowers stolen from the centerpieces. A friend from the pool told me that I was strong, that I would get through this, and I was confused. Strong? I wondered silently. What does this have to do with swimming?

I had told Paul that when I died I wanted to be cremated and my ashes tossed into Paradox Lake. "Don't you want to be somewhere, so people can visit your grave?" he asked me.

"I don't mind. You can do whatever you want with me. I'll be beyond caring. How about you? What would you want?"

And he would never answer, never talk about it, just as he would never sign the organ-donor part of his driver's license, or tell me what he thought of me when we met. I'll never know if I made this up, but I had this memory of him looking out our window in Paradox, out at the field, and saying, "This would be a nice place to be buried, I suppose."

So on this day I walked our land, looking from all angles, trying to see the valley and the mountains through my tears, as our families waited in our home. Like a dowser searching for water, I sought to divine the perfect spot, a place where I could keep my eye on Paul's grave from the house, but not so close that I wouldn't be able to avoid seeing it when I didn't want to face it. The view from the burial place needed to be beautiful, sweeping, majestic. Our friends Bob and Marie waited quietly with the oak sapling they had uprooted. Paul had told me a story once as we strolled through the woods on Schroon Lake. It was early spring and an Indian maiden had been promised in marriage to an old chief, but she was in love with a young, handsome brave. Upset, in a panic, she ran into the forest. "O mighty oak," she wailed, "what should I do? I am in love with one man and my father is trying to force me to marry another!"

"Go to your father, my child," said the mighty oak, "and tell him that you will marry the chief when the last leaf falls from the old oak in the forest. I will do what I can for you."

The young woman did as she was told and her father agreed to wait, willing to allow her one last summer of youthful freedom. Autumn came, the nights got colder and then the days. The leaves of all the other trees turned fiery with brilliant abandon and fell to the ground. But the mighty oak held on to his leaves, even as they dried and faded to a brittle brown. Throughout the winter, through the wind and the snow, there were leaves left to prove the oak's constancy, and the maiden's. When spring finally arrived with new buds to replenish the last of the tired leaves, the father relented, knowing that the oak had endured, and allowed the daughter to marry her true love.

I wanted such a tree to watch over Paul when I couldn't be there, so he would never be alone in the middle of that field. But it was the wrong time of year to transplant an oak tree, and the sapling hasn't thrived.

It was hot and heavy and humid. A storm was on the way, but until it arrived the air was oppressive, the haze ever so languidly thickening into dense clouds. And still, I shivered with cold. A small group of friends and relatives stood, heads bowed, gathered around a ragged hole in the ground beside the newly planted oak. Before the ceremony, one of our friends asked if I would like music, he had brought his guitar. Sometimes when we spent evenings with friends in Paradox, someone would play a piano, or pull out a guitar, and, after a few standards, ask for requests. Paul persistently asked to hear a song that he insisted he knew from his boyhood in Colorado called "On the Trail of the Lonesome Pine," but no one had ever heard of it, we thought he made it up. It was all I could think of at the time, but of course our friend still didn't know it, so "Scarlet Ribbons" was sung instead. It took me several years, but I finally found Paul's song. It was actually the title of a novel by John Fox, Jr., which was twice made into a silent movie before becoming the first film to be shot outdoors in color. The title song from the movie was "Twilight on the Trail," and it was supposedly one of F.D.R.'s two favorite songs. I can't imagine how Paul came across it. These are the words:

When it's twilight on the trail
And I jog along
The world is like a dream,
And the ripple of the stream
Is my song.

When it's twilight on the trail
And I rest once more
My ceiling is the sky,
And the grass on which I lie
Is my floor.

Never ever have a nickel in my jeans
Never ever have a debt to pay,
Still I understand what real contentment means.
Guess I was born that way.

When it's twilight on the trail
And my voice is still
Please plant this heart of mine
Underneath the lonesome pine on the hill.
When it's twilight on the trail.

I met the minister who conducted the ceremony for the first time a short while before the service. A neighbor had arranged to have him there; otherwise, no one would have known what to do or say. He was tentative, unsure of himself. I didn't want anything too religious, or anything too personal, since he had never met Paul. He asked me if I minded if he quoted the bit from Ecclesiastes about there being a time and a season for everything. I bristled, but he quickly said he wanted to add that this was not the time for this to have happened, not the season. I agreed, making him promise to say the last bit, the part not in the Bible, for I refused to allow anyone to assert that this was meant to be, and weeks later was to scream obscenities at someone who did.

Our land is part of a long field cradled in a valley with a stream running through it. When the minister read, 'Yea, though I walk through the valley of the shadow of death . . ." I thought, This is it, that exact valley. Our house was originally part of a school for disturbed adolescents and on the crest of the next hill, almost a mile away, is the grave of a boy. He had a seizure in a lake while on a class outing and drowned. His parents didn't want his body, so he was buried on school property, his name carved into a large rock. But the valley is too beautiful, it can hold its own against the sorrow. In a time long ago, it was a seabed. Not far beneath the topsoil is pure, fine sand. Along with Paul's ashes, I buried a small jar of mementos, a wallet-size copy of our wedding picture, the few souvenirs I could bear to part with. It was as if I didn't want even his ashes to be alone.

We moved inside the house as the clouds extinguished the sun. The neighbors had cleaned; the wooden table was buried beneath platters of food. There were flowers everywhere, formal bouquets transported from the city and bunches of wildflowers gathered from the fields. The windows and doors were open, even after the wind blew through, spraying water droplets into the room. My sister stood in the doorway, holding her infant daughter, showing her rain for the first time in her short life, as Los Angeles, where they lived, was in the midst of a drought. Paul's father said to me, "There will be a rainbow afterwards. You'll see." But there wasn't. And I was annoyed with him for thinking there could be, or that it would matter if there was, that anything could appease. Conversations trailed off. There was really nothing to say. The rain drumming on the tin roof drowned out the silence.

AUGUST 15, 1990

Everyone has finally gone. My parents wanted to stay, but I wouldn't let them. The sound of voices grates unbearably on my exposed nerves, the presence of others drives me deeper into myself. The shock has been woven into a heavy blanket of sadness under which I burrow. I take my sleeping pill in the early evening, hating nothing more than waking in the morning. The bright sunshine is a personal affront. One morning, as I am lying in bed trying desperately to hang on to sleep, a neighbor knocks at my front door. She sees my car. She knows I am inside. I look out my bedroom window, then crawl back under the covers when I see who it is. She knocks again. Silence. Then she tries the door. I am enraged, overwhelmed by anger at her audacity. "Leave me alone!" I want to scream. "Go away!" rises in my throat. But instead I lie trembling under the quilt until, finally, she drives away. I cannot abide the concern of others. They do nothing for me except remind me what it must be like for them, to go home to their safe families.

There is an asterisk on this day in Paul's datebook. I don't know why. One week ago today . . .

A U G U S T   1 8 ,   1 9 9 0

I hike to Gooseneck Pond, armed with stationery and a pen. There are letters that must be written, people who need to be told; most important, Aunt Mildred and Uncle Edgar. I sit on a rock staring out at the burnished waves, composing myself in between sentences. These people took us into their hearts, and though we spent only a few days together out of our entire lives, the bonds are true, and I know how my letter will devastate them, they who married so late in life yet spent so many happy years together. I try to cushion the blow, both in my opening words and by writing on the outside of the envelope,

"Caution. This letter contains very bad news." They did not have a telephone, I did not know how else to do it. When Aunt Mildred wrote back, she told me they thought the bad news was that we weren't coming over, that I wasn't going to swim the English Channel after all, that it would be a long time before they saw us again. They weren't prepared, how could they have been, and it hit them hard. Several years later, when Aunt Mildred wrote to tell me of Uncle Edgar's death, most of her compassion was still for me, for how much worse my lot had been, for Paul had been so young, and had died so suddenly, when we should have had so much ahead of us. She and I are brought closer by widowhood, although I have yet to see her again.

I call to check our answering machine in New York, and catch myself hoping there will be a message from Paul.

AUGUST 20, 1990

I cannot sit still; I cannot move. I keep thinking if I do something, go somewhere, this will stop, this soul-searing anguish that finds no solace. A friend of mine owns a weekend house on a lake in Pennsylvania. He is one of those who have offered to do anything they can, and would do it unobtrusively. I borrow his cabin in the middle of the week, when no one is around.

Paul and I had been there together. The first time was early in our relationship, in the middle of our first winter. The water hibernated under a solid crust of ice. There were four or five of us, my friends from swimming. We walked out on the lake shortly after sunset to look for a comet that was supposed to be visible at dusk. The sky was a luminescent indigo, the horizon a glowing magenta. We were all intently, seriously, scanning the sky. It had become quite cold; our feet painfully crunched ice crystals. No one wanted to be the first to give up, but we were all chilled and bored and ready to go inside. All of a sudden Paul shouted, "I see it! There it is!" pointing to what was quite obviously an airplane. We laughed, our breath as white as snow. Someone else pointed out another comet/airplane. Satisfied, happy, joking about a sky filled with comets, we ran and slid across the lake, back into the light and warmth.

The days seem even longer in Pennsylvania. I cannot fill the time. Memories torture me; I have not fled far enough. One morning when I walked out the front door I found some religious tracts someone had left, about death and salvation. I was horified. Was it some kind of frightful coincidence? I called the friend whose house it was. Had such a thing ever happened before? Was there some perverse religious sect in the area that went around leaving potentially upsetting literature at the houses of strangers? He was startled at first, then extremely apologetic. He had told the next-door neighbors of my situation, and that I would be staying at his house. He never expected that they would disturb my privacy.

Paul and I had spent a weekend in this house earlier in the summer, just before the Montauk swim. I hadn't been crazy about being there, because the lake is small, only about a half mile across, which made any long swims boring. But we were doing a mini-taper anyway—just a few days of lighter than normal yardage. The lake was nice because there were no motor-boats, but Paul paddled along anyway; it was what we were accustomed to. That evening, I don't know why, I guess I had just received my new driver's license, I filled out the organ-donation questions, and Paul, in spite of my urging, refused to do the same, just shrugged it off. I didn't think to ask him why. He spent a lot of time that night trying to fix a videotape. Maybe that's all it was, he didn't want the interruption. Or maybe, like all young men, although surely he was old enough to know better, he thought himself immortal. Or maybe he wouldn't have wanted to admit he believed in being buried intact. Surely it couldn't have been that.

The next day we went to an antiques store at the end of a dirt road. The shop was housed in several outbuildings of what had once been a farm, all painted red wood with peeling white trim. Mottled sunlight did little to illuminate the insides of the buildings; the windows were too dusty. Instead, feeble electric lights were lit in the middle of the day, but still it was dark and cool inside, and hushed. There was no one else there. We spent what seemed like hours poking around, searching for treasures. We bought two things, one more or less Paul's, one mine. His was an odd, old fire extinguisher, a frosted glass globe filled with some unknown liquid nestled in an aluminum cylinder. It was made to attach to a wall. Apparently, the glass was meant to shatter and the magic liquid, surely not just water, would put out the fire. We never exactly figured out how it would work, but we liked the look of it. My object was a copper canister, worn and old, and, for some reason which I've forgotten, more appealing to me than anything else there. I barely remember what it looked like; I had it for so short a time. I buried Paul's ashes in it.

I was finding that I couldn't bear to be anywhere we had been together, or, more accurately, couldn't bear to be. Several people had suggested at the funeral that I swim the English Channel sometime in the future as a memorial to Paul. They didn't understand about the cold. I knew that I could never go through the training again without him, but it started to seem that if I could do it that same summer, then Paul would really be along, in a way he could never be again. I figured that no pain I inflicted on myself would be as severe as that which I was experiencing, so I had nothing to lose. If I couldn't die, I could at least swim the English Channel.

AUGUST 23, 1990

On this date in Paul's calendar is written "Sal to US/ PC to US." It was tentative, this plan, based on the assumption that we would have had good weather and the pilot could have made space for us in his schedule. We were willing to stay longer. I would no doubt have accompanied Paul to Birmingham, not wanting to travel back to New York alone. The only way he was able to book the flight with his frequent-flier miles was in business class, and that ticket was mine; he would be in coach, as he always was when the company paid. We joked about his visiting me in the fancy part of the plane, maybe even trying to boast his way into business class by telling the flight

127

attendant that I had just swum the English Channel, and wasn't it a shame that he wasn't sitting next to me for the ride home.

Instead, on this date, I go to the store to buy black clothes. It seems so shallow, to go shopping at such a time, but I do not wish to wear anything but black. In the dresser drawers stay the muted grays and greens, the teals and plums. The colors of my clothes had never been bright but they appeared garish to me now. I am a widow. I will wear black. In New York City, this color is fashionable, favored by many women, so that it is impossible to tell those in mourning from those who are simply chic.

AUGUST 25, 1990

I drove back upstate, where Brian and Gregg accompanied me on yet another nine-mile swim of Schroon Lake. They didn't ask why, thinking, no doubt, it was some kind of memorial, not knowing that it was to reassure myself that although I had barely swum, or eaten, for two and a half weeks, I had not lost too much speed or endurance. It had surely started to cool off as autumn approached, but I don't recall being cold. I'm sure it was the most difficult swim I've ever done in my life, but I barely remember it. I concentrated on not thinking about who was in that boat, and who wasn't. In blocking so much from my mind during that swim, I lost the memory of the swim as well, except for the very beginning, when the prescription goggles were wasted; they fogged and blurred too easily. I have a dim recollection of that choking, suffocating sensation people must feel when they're drowning. But I hypnotized myself with the rhythm of the swimming, and the waves, and emptied my mind until I walked up the sandy beach, among children and sunbathers and strangers. Afterwards I sat on the dock, absorbing the heat from the sun-baked planks, wrapped in towels, in misery, miles away from the people moving around me, tying the canoe onto the luggage rack, loading the gear into the car. Brian, who had swum beside me for a little while, assured me, when I asked, that no, I hadn't been too slow, it was a good pace.

I phoned the boat pilot in England. He was hesitant, but I wasn't listening, talked over his objections. He agreed to see what he could do if I showed up. Those were the words I heard.

A U G U S T 2 7 , 1 9 9 0

The first time I swam around Manhattan, I had trained heavily. The evening before the day of the race, the boat I had booked broke down and backed out. I spent the night on the phone trying unsuccessfully to find another one. Luckily, when I arrived the next morning, a man with a Boston Whaler was there waiting, hoping to make a little money if a swimmer needed a boat at the last minute. I felt that I hadn't swum my best that day and didn't know if it was the anxiety of the night before or if maybe I had overtrained, not rested enough. When I was approached about breaking the women's record, a month or so later, I worried that I was already out of shape. Even though

I had continued to work out all summer, my mileage had been cut back. There was still a certain amount of intense pain, and the water was way too warm for me, but throughout most of that second trip around Manhattan, I felt strong and fast and wonderful. I convinced myself that I could do just as well now, that even though my English Channel training had come to a screeching halt, it was like money in the bank, and still available to me.

It never occurred to me that the hours spent curled up on my bed, sobbing, the hours spent in the heaviness of drug-induced sleep, the hours that were lost, never to be found, would affect my swimming ability. I existed in a state where mind and body were separate, in constant conflict with each other. When fatigue overwhelmed my limbs, my thoughts raced. When drowsiness soothed my tortured mind, my body persisted in tossing and turning in frenetic rebellion. I convinced myself that I could count on the physical to take charge. I may not have been able to think clearly, but surely I would still be able to swim as long as I needed to.

SEPTEMBER 4, 1990

I changed the unused plane ticket and was due to fly to London the next day. I wanted one more morning swim in Paradox before driving down to New York. The fog was thick and heavy, inpenetrable; I was impatient, ready to move on. I waited until as late as I thought I could and then decided to swim, no matter that I could barely see, figuring that if I just swam straight out from the beach, parallel to the almost discernible trees, and then turned around where the lake opened up from the cove, I'd be fine.

So I did exactly that, or thought I did, but when I got back to the shore, I had no idea where I was. I wasn't scared. I could see land, however unrecognizable the location may have been. What became more and more upsetting to me was the fear that I would be forced to knock on someone's door, dripping wet and shivering, to ask where I was. Instead, I kept swimming, first in the direction that felt right, then in the opposite direction, until finally out of the mist loomed the beach house I sought. It was little mishaps like this that whirled me into a rage of grief, that reminded me that my life no longer revolved around anything familiar, that at the center was still, as always, Paul, but that all else had spun out of control, a vortex around a vacuum. Simple things, like swimming there and back, were no longer simple. The tears flowed into lake water and mist droplets until I no longer knew what dampened my cheeks as I ran to my car, as I drove home.

I flew to London in the pampered comfort of business class. Turning my face toward the window, I closed my eyes and tried to evaporate into the starry night. Paul had this idea he wanted to sell to the airlines. He would print a card or a booklet that would fit into the seat pocket which had various cloud formations pictured, with names and basic information. It would be a way for bored passengers to learn something as they stared out into the sky, a way to distract fidgety children. He hadn't thought, or hadn't told me, of adding constellations for those like me, fleeing through the darkness.

The train ride to Dover was simple. I had made a reservation somewhere other than where we had planned to stay. The room looked out on the Channel, the coast of France easily visible, glowing in the late-afternoon light. Surely that would make it easier, being able to see the land for myself, not to be forced to rely on someone else to reassure me that it was just ahead.

S E P T E M B E R   8 ,   1 9 9 0

I forgot there was going to be that last bit of training when I got there—becoming familiar once more with unknown waters. This is barely cold, I thought initially, amazed. This would have been absolutely possible. It took only one dolphin dive off the bottom to get started, that's how warm it was. No ice-cold headaches, no need for a second try. And yet, after swimming for forty minutes, I was unable to stop shivering. The next day I could endure only twenty minutes. It wasn't the water temperature. I could barely get out of bed in the morning—how did I ever think I would be able to swim along a beach without Paul walking beside me? My attention span was too short. It was only possible to swim for as long as the activity distracted me; as soon as I got used to it, I had to move on to something else—reading a book, walking a few miles, riding a train to Canterbury. I was impatient for time to pass, and anything that took too long reminded me of what lay ahead, and what remained behind, and the interminable gap between the two.

One afternoon, when I was still thinking I might do this swim, I sat on the beach, hiding in my towel after having swum several times back and forth across the harbor. My head bowed, resting on my raised knees, I was oblivious to my surroundings. I heard a woman say, "Excuse me," and I looked up. "Are you swimming the Channel?" she asked, then, perhaps because I looked startled, or alarmed, "It's just that most people swimming here now, like you were just doing, are training for the Channel."

"I was going to, but something happened, and now I'm not," I somehow blurted out. And I knew then I wouldn't. Letting go of the Channel turned out to be the easiest thing I did that summer, barely worthy of regret. I was beyond caring. It was without meaning in the context of what had been, and what would never be. I could not put so much effort into an endeavor born in youth and optimism, qualities that were so distant now, infinitely farther than the few miles between England and France. Besides, the promise I had made to Paul, that I wouldn't do it without him, haunted me. What hadn't seemed like a deathbed promise at the time felt like one now. Swimming was no longer something that was mine alone, it had become his as well, and I gave him this particular swim, let him take it away with him. If we couldn't share it, I wanted no part of it. To do it as a memorial to him would prove that I could do it without him, and this I was unwilling to do. I was fooling myself, thinking he would be there, beside me, with me. He was gone.

I phoned the boat pilot to tell him my decision. He was not surprised; he had thought it a foolish idea, although he didn't actually say so. He tried to give me advice, as only those who don't know could, to say that my way of dealing with things wasn't good, that I should be on holiday with friends, instead of on my own. He said it sounded like I was ready to throw myself from a bridge. As if that wouldn't be the most stupid way to do it, for a swimmer. He was trying to be kind, I suppose, but mostly I tuned him out, as I had already learned to do, until he said, in response to some long-forgotten words of mine, "It sounds like you were very lucky to have had what very few people in this world ever experience."

I cross the English Channel on the hydrofoil, that peculiar boat/helicopter hybrid that skims the surface of the water. I sit by a window, but it is impossible to see through the salt-encrusted glass.

The thing is, I don't want to swim the English Channel without Paul any more than I want to live without Paul. Life as I knew it and loved it is over. I want to volunteer to play a role in the next senseless killing—to be the next innocent bystander shot on a city street, the next random victim of a terrorist's bomb. I don't have the will to kill myself, but I have no desire to go on. When I was in New York after Paul died, I watched people cross the street and I thought, Why couldn't it have been you? You look like a jerk, why should you make it to the other side? You can't possibly deserve to live as much as he did. Now I just want to sacrifice myself, not out of nobility, but because it seems logical. Instead of some husband or wife having to learn this grief, why not just let me take their place?

I play the "time game" a lot. It started while Paul was in the hospital. This time four hours ago, my life was still perfect. This time two days ago, Paul was still alive. This time a month and a day ago, I had just kissed Paul goodbye. If time is indeed a river, as the physicists like to say, why can't I swim upstream?

I force myself to remember what he looked like in the hospital—the black eyes, the bandaged head, the swollen face, the tubes—to convince myself that he's really gone. I wish I had thought to ask for a lock of his hair, to put in the locket he gave me when we married, but probably it had all been shaven. I try to conjure up what it felt like to be held by him, to be kissed by him, to touch him, to be comforted by him. I am so afraid of forgetting, but I can't bear to remember. My life is an enormous, aching void that I don't know how to fill, so I just travel on.

I spend the night in Paris. I had forgotten how beautiful this city is, the cream-colored confections of buildings swirled through with wrought iron, the narrow river traversed by ancient stone bridges. I am reminded of why I chose to live here more than a dozen years ago, and why I wanted to bring Paul here, to show him. Another thing to add to the ever-growing list of regrets.

I wonder if a day will ever pass without tears, especially given the way that days now linger. Or if I will ever laugh again, a real laugh, a laugh-till-I-cry laugh. Once Paul and I went on a hike to Pharaoh Lake. It was my idea, as usual. I had this crazy idea about swimming in all the lakes in the Adirondacks, and this one had made its way to the top of my list. The trail went for quite a distance past swampland, skirting bogs and stagnant pools of water, through squishy mud that made sucking noises as it tried to devour our hiking boots. The air was dense with mosquitoes massed in a feeding frenzy. We were trying new bug repellant which turned out to be ineffectual. We grabbed the largest ferns we found, swatting when we could, waving them through the air the rest of the time. As I hit myself, I chanted, "Mea culpa, mea culpa. I'm so sorry. I promise I'll let you choose all the hikes from now on. I'm sorry. It was a horrible idea, and it was mine. Mea culpa." We laughed as we ran through the woods until the trail was too steep, at which point we panted and swatted and sweated in silence.

At the end of the hike there always comes a time when more and more sky is visible through the trees, assuming that the destination is either a mountaintop or a lake. Our spirits rose with the elevation. The mosquitoes fell away with the shade and we emerged into a bowl of sunlight, squinting in the dazzling light, the breeze off the water whisking away our sweat as the sun gently warmed us dry.

We immediately took off our shoes and socks to feel the coolness of earth and rock, to check for blisters. We waded into the soothing water together, only to find that the fish were very, very hungry. They swarmed around our feet, nibbling on our toes. It was absolutely disgusting. As we ate our lunch, we threw crumbs for them. The water swirled and bubbled as the fish snapped up the food. We assured each other that there had never been any reports of piranhas in the Adirondacks. I put off swimming as long as I could, finally immersing myself more quickly than I ever had, diving past the shallow water, kicking and splashing to scare the fish away. They weren't more than a couple inches long, but still . . . They didn't follow me into the deeper water.

Eventually I swam back to where Paul was calmly reading. I treaded water, looking anxiously around. "Honey," I called. "Could you try to distract the fish while I swim in and get out?" meaning, of course, that he should throw some crumbs in at a distance from me.

"Sure, li'l Sal," he said in his goofy mode, which should have warned me. "I'll do that for you." He walked a few feet over from the shallow rock where I would walk out, and stood there, looking down. I took a deep breath and thrashed my way in. All of a sudden, when I neared the rock, the fish made a beeline for me, surrounded me, nipped at my heels, my legs, my arms. I pulled myself, in a panic, out of the water.

"Why weren't you throwing food for them? I thought you were going to distract them!"

"I tried," Paul protested. "I was telling them fish stories."

Just to make me laugh.

SEPTEMBER 11, 1990

I arrived in Biarritz, remembering it as being a sleepy dowager of a seaside resort, having spent a November day here the year of my travels through Europe. I had assumed that by September the summer crowds would be gone, but I was wrong. I found myself in the middle of a film festival, complete with traffic jams, endlessly honking horns, and hordes of tanned, beautiful people. The heat baked the town into a pungent mix of automobile exhaust, suntan lotion, and cooking food, all of which repulsed me, leaving me queasy. I couldn't wait to escape. Back in New York, I had gone through my Michelin guide, and other resources, seeking the perfect, quiet, medieval seaside town. There was some innate survival sense telling me that as long as I was going to be miserable, I might as well be miserable someplace beautiful. I loved Brittany but was afraid that it would be too cool and dreary in September, so I looked farther south. Biarritz might be too crowded, but St.-Jean-de-Luz sounded like the perfect alternative. I had never been there, but if it was worse than where I was, I could always move on. Staying where I was out of a fear of the unknown seemed stupid. I went to the bustling, overworked tourist office in Biarritz to book a room there for the next night. They found me a hotel that wasn't in my guidebook, which worried me. But I was too tired, and too afraid of breaking down in public, to do anything but accept. I was actually proud of myself. I was hot, tired, and discouraged, but I did not cry until I was alone in my hotel room.

I am tormented by the sounds of talking and laughter and glasses clinking that invade my room through the window, until at long last the sleeping pill weaves its spell. It is still light outside.

SEPTEMBER 12, 1990

 I've been racing nonstop in an attempt to forget what day it is. I swam in the ocean at Biarritz, entranced by the weird rock formations growing out of the sand, ran errands, took the bus down the coast to St.-Jean-de-Luz, and it's still the same morning. It is beautiful here, the hotel perfect. No one is particularly nice to me, but that's okay. I don't want anyone to know and have no more interest in talking to them than they in talking to me. It feels as though I have a shameful secret to hide. I don't want to see the horrified looks, the fear, the pity.

The main part of the hotel is on a cliff; my room is on the second floor in one of the little cottages clustered off to one side, floating on clouds of hydrangeas, a flower that once seemed fussy and old-fashioned but that I have come to love. The petals are a full palette of sea and sky, viridian bleeding into ultramarine fading into violet. My French windows open out over the Atlantic, the scent of the sea wafts in on the breeze. The room has two twin beds covered with ragged fuchsia chenille spreads, in opposite corners, and a battered wooden table with two chairs, a bathroom without a shower, and a telephone.

A paved path winds its way from high over the hissing, roiling ocean down to the beach. The calmness of the bay is in extreme contrast to the violent pounding beyond the sheltered confines of the cove. There is a long crescent of sand; one can swim about half a mile parallel to the shore before reaching the other side. The town lies upstage of the beach. Lumpy cobblestone streets flow into steps; ancient stone houses with shuttered windows echo with the ghosts of summers past. Although it is autumn, there are still a fair number of tourists, or maybe it's the townspeople who fill the streets and restaurants. I try not to see them, the happy couples as they sit at the outdoor café tables overflowing with plates of seafood, bottles of wine, good cheer.

I have traveled far and wide on my own but never mastered the knack of eating by myself in a restaurant. I felt too self-conscious, too obviously alone. And that was before. Instead, I go to the charcuterie and buy a container of paella to take back to my room, to eat with a plastic fork, and wash it down with wine, or cider, anything that contains alcohol.

I find myself unable to think about Paul—my mind shies away from him, another survival instinct. Don't think about it, I tell myself. Wait until each memory no longer rips its way through your heart. Besides, I don't need to think about him, I try to convince myself, he is no longer separate from who I am. I cannot think of who this new person is, or is going to become. It is too soon to know. I am angry at him for not being more wary, for not loving me enough to be more careful for my sake, for assuming people stop when the light turns red, for being annoyed at me all those times I pulled him back from the curb. He died not knowing these things could happen, and I resent that. I fear my bitterness, and sense that it is a feeble attempt to make my grief manageable, to transform it into a simpler emotion.

Paul's mother died the year before we were married. A week after the funeral, as Paul's father was leaving the cemetery he made a left turn. There was a blind spot in the road, a hill, and a young man on a motorcycle did not see the car until it was too late. He swerved and lost control. He died, leaving a young wife and a child. At the time, our sympathy was overwhelmingly for Paul's father, what a traumatic thing to happen to him on the way home from his wife's grave, from the horror of newly shoveled dirt. I remember thinking of the motorcyclist, Well, if he had really loved his wife, he would have worn a helmet. Now I know better and am ashamed.

It was four years after Paul died that I truly understood how these things happen, so suddenly, so absolutely without warning. I was in Paradox, standing on a neighbor's lawn, visiting with a group of people. There was a large dog, a Rottweiler, tied with a long rope to a tree. He saw or heard another dog down the hill, and took off running as we all watched. No one realized that I was in a dangerous position. As the rope pulled taut, it caught me across the back of the legs, and because the dog was so big and so strong, the force of the line stopping flipped me several feet into the air. I landed flat on my back, unable to move, or breathe, the wind knocked out of me. In an instant, I was gasping for air, crying from the shock and the pain.

At home, it hit me that this was how, on a bright, sunny day, in the midst of people who remained untouched, disaster could pick a body up and throw it to the ground, as if it were a rag doll instead of a human being. And there was no way to resist, no chance to break the fall, no opportunity to fight back, to grab on to life. It happens too fast, in no time at all. I had been in accidents before—for instance, a ladder, with me on the top, had fallen over while I was focusing a light in a theatre. But whenever one is in a vaguely precarious position, like high in the air, perched on a few thin pieces of aluminum, one senses that something could go wrong at any time, and is tensed in preparation. Had I been seriously injured, it wouldn't have been so inexplicable. Even being struck by lightning mustn't come totally out of the blue, as it happens during a thunderstorm, and the possibility of such a thing occurring is the underlying reason that severe weather is exciting. I suppose, well, I know, that crossing a New York City street is not so innocuous as standing in an idyllic lakeside setting, but I understood, in a way I hadn't before, how it must have been.

It is the afternoon of my thirty-fifth birthday. I am sitting on a rock, watching the sea, letting the Atlantic Ocean wash away my sorrow. It is perhaps a mistake to make birthdays special in the life of a child; it renders them so difficult in the life of an adult. I have a rule in my life, and even now I don't break it. I must swim on my birthday, preferably outside, in open water. My morning swim in Biarritz wasn't enough today; this afternoon I swam in the protected cove in St.-Jean-de-Luz.

For a year and a half I worked on the Macy's Thanksgiving Day parade. Macy's had a company policy that employees could take their birthday, or a day of their choice within thirty days of their birthday, as a day off, a paid holiday. Paul and I kept to that tradition as best we could in our years together, although I haven't had a job since then where I got any sort of paid leave, and was no longer working there when we met. My thirty-third birthday fell on a Monday, so we spent a long weekend upstate. I requested that we camp out Sunday night, so I could awaken at my favorite place to swim in the Adirondacks, Gooseneck Pond. It's off the beaten track, about a half hour's hike into the woods, and the first little bit is across private land posted with No Trespassing signs. I always figure they don't mean me. The "pond" (it would be considered a lake anywhere but the Adirondacks with its plethora of lakes) was formed by a glacier slicing a swath through a mountain. Sienna and ocher cliffs plunge straight down into clear, almost turquoise water. Wind-gnarled pine trees somehow hang on to precarious perches on what appears to be sheer rock. Hawks circle high overhead, loons disturb the peace with their madcap cries. I once saw a snapping turtle swimming frantically out of my way, far below me, after which I always tried to remember to be careful as I walked into the water.

We had borrowed an inflatable boat, sleeping bags, and a tent. The plan was to load all the gear and Paul into the boat, so he could paddle to the other end while I swam. I had my heart set on camping at the far side, just over a mile away as the crow flies, or the fish swims. When we reached the water, there was a stiff breeze and whitecaps. Paul thought he should have a head start because he sensed rough going and didn't want me there ahead of him, waiting, shivering, until he arrived with my dry towel. But the boat was too light and Paul was blown around in circles. He fought his way back to shore, frustrated and annoyed.

"We'll have to walk there."

"I could swim and pull you in the boat," I offered.

"No. It's too rough. We'll just put everything back in the packs and walk."

There was no trail to the other end. We bushwhacked through the underbrush, sometimes wandering far into the woods to go around ravines, hiking a much greater distance than if we had traveled by water. Paul, in spite of his years as a Boy Scout, was not a happy camper. The wet rubber boat that had been too light was now too heavy. I felt guilty, dragging Paul into something he obviously wasn't enjoying. We argued practically the whole way about nothing. The sky was gray and dreary, the wind added an unpleasant chill. But when the darkness of the forest finally opened onto the steely gleam of the water, the beauty overwhelmed the anger. We both apologized, chagrined. Arriving was a relief, the journey forgotten. We sat on the smooth rock high above the pond, arms around each other, and enjoyed the view. After setting up the tent, we ate dinner and watched the moon rise across the water. The clouds crept in behind us and we fell asleep, snuggled in the coziness of sleeping bags zipped together, to the soothing patter of a light rain.

The next morning we packed up beneath a fresh, clear sky, preparing to do the reverse of the trip we hadn't done the evening before, this time both of us in a much better mood. Once again I waited, huddled on a rock, shivering in bathing suit, cap, and goggles, while Paul started to paddle back. I was about to ask him why he was staying so close to the shore, to suggest that maybe it wasn't such a great idea, when he found out for himself, snagging the boat on an underwater branch. He hadn't gotten very far. I half swam, half ran through the water to him. While he tried to hold his finger over the hole, I emptied the boat of our gear, splashing my way back and forth to land, then dragged the boat, with Paul still in it, fully clothed and barely wet, to where he could disembark on the shore. I have to admit I was laughing the whole time, Paul repeating over and over, "Thank you. You saved my life, li'l Sal! I would have drowned without you!" I didn't point out that he wouldn't have been in that situation without me, and that the water was no more than three feet deep.

We had a patch kit for the boat and fixed it in a flash. There was no way either of us would give up at this point, so we hit the water one more time. I had a lovely birthday swim—cool, choppy, and bracing. Paul stayed fairly close in the boat—I'm not sure for his sake or mine—so we arrived together, packed our gear, and laughed our way down the trail. Is it only in retrospect that all arguments ended in laughter? I fear that I glaze my memories with a rose-colored wash, erasing the times that anger lasted, painting an unrealistic picture of our life together. Yet it is the life I remember, and I would swear it was real.

It is finally sunset, signaling the end of this overlong day. I am sitting on the edge of a cliff with a tiny ledge perfectly placed for my feet—a hundred feet above fingers of rock that reach into the foaming sea. The thundering force, even from this distance, is terrifying, as the waves explode into plumes of white spray. It is difficult to believe that all that noise is nothing more than air bubbles shattering as the water hits the shore. Birds fly below me. I am barely nervous. I don't know if the cliff is eroded away beneath me, if I am on a promontory too weak to support my weight, and I don't care. People walking by on the path lean over to look, making those peculiar French clucking sounds or gasping, "Ooh la!" but they seem to sense that it would not serve to say anything to me.

I would have two regrets if I were to crash to the rocks below—the first, that it would be difficult for my parents to deal with everything in a foreign country. My father's high-school French would hardly suffice. The second would be that it hadn't happened one month and four days earlier. I might be afraid of feeling something, of lying there hurt but alive. They said that Paul wouldn't have felt anything, that it happened instantly, but what if it didn't, how do they know—how do they know he was really dead if they could make him breathe and make his heart beat and make him pull back his toe when they pushed on it? I have this fantasy that they hid him in the basement of the hospital and did some quasi-scientific experiment to give him a new brain, and someday they will call me and tell me that he is as good as new, come get him. It would be fine if he looked a bit like Frankenstein's monster, with weird scars and bumps; it may have been his appearance that initially attracted me, but it wasn't what made me love him.

I am unable to jump from here but I cannot help but hope that the ledge will crumble away beneath me. My birthday wish is death. I am, if nothing else, realistic in my hopes and dreams. I know by now it is useless to wish to have Paul back. This is what I tell myself, but in my weakest, most needy moments, I cannot help myself.

My parents call, my sister calls. No one actually says, "Happy birthday." They are smarter than that. But they let me know they know, and are grieving for me.

Alone in my hotel room, now that the sun has finally set, I bury my face in Paul's shirt. I thought myself lucky because, although I had done laundry the day he died, I had missed one article of clothing, which had fallen behind a chair. Long after the last of his scent had evaporated from his pillowcase, I could still smell his sweat on that one precious shirt. I brought it along to France with me in a plastic bag, making sure to seal it back up each night before I fall asleep, careful not to wash away his essence with my tears.

Feeling myself to be an exile in a foreign country suits my frame of mind. If I don't concentrate, the French language rolls over me in a senseless wave. There is a certain appeal to being an expatriate. Simple chores, such as buying food or aspirin, become accomplishments. And these errands are the extent of my social intercourse. I have no desire to talk to anyone; the rudimentaries of letting a stranger know me would be too much and I have no interest in anyone else, unless they have been through what I have and know some shortcuts, although I sense there are none. I wouldn't believe anyone who told me there is an easy way through this, as much as I wish there were.

I had a nightmare about a shortcut once. It was in the weeks before the race around Manhattan. I dreamed that, while swimming up the Harlem River, I turned left at 125th Street, where a canal had recently been cut through the island, all the way to the Hudson River. About halfway across, I realized what I had done and that it was cheating. In a panic, I tried to turn around, even though it meant backtracking and losing time. I knew the swim wouldn't count unless it was done right. But, try as I might, I couldn't go back, couldn't force my body to swim in the direction my mind wanted it to go, couldn't beat the current that was sweeping me along the wrong way. Waves slapped the smooth cement walls which rose high on either side, like a prison. I screamed at the people in my boat, how could they allow me to do such a thing, trying to place blame, even though I knew it was my fault, guilt strangling me. Flailing my arms, gasping for air, I fought to return, until I woke, in a sweat, the sheets twisted into a straitjacket.

Every evening I take my notebook to the cliff, to watch the sunset. I haven't kept a diary since I was a young girl, and never for longer than a few days, but now I feel compelled to write things down even though they may be too painful to ever read. Writing and tears are my safety valves when pressure builds. Speech is beyond my capability. I talk to myself or to Paul, and either way, the words need not be spoken. It is as if those hours spent face down in lakes and pools and seas were not preparing me for the English Channel but for this long stretch of quiet in a different sort of saltwater.

The sun burns out once again in a blaze of glory. I kept watch over one particular rosy cloud, telling myself it was Paul, until I could no longer see, lost him. But then it came back in a final burst—the only bright spot left in a muted sky of mauve and dusty gray. The problem is, I don't believe in life after death, but now I see why so many people do, and wish I did. If I could think of Paul somewhere with wings and a halo watching me, it wouldn't be nearly so lonely. Instead, all I believe is left of him is what's inside me, the memories, the mark he made on this world when he was here. It would feel like cheating if I changed my beliefs to fit the situation, and maybe he is more alive my way. Every breath I take is his as well.

Three years after Paul died I drove from Pittsburgh to New York during what was being billed as the Blizzard of the Century. Something like two or three feet of snow fell in about twelve hours. I thought if I started early I could at least make it partway, then pull off the highway and stay somewhere if the predictions came true. The weather reports advised staying home but, if it was absolutely necessary to travel, to take supplies in case you were stranded. I brought barely any food, and one thermos of coffee—but plenty to read. When I left my parents' apartment at 6:30 a.m., there was already a certain accumulation. As I traveled east on the Pennsylvania Turnpike, through the mountains, for long stretches of time mine was the only vehicle. I later discovered that the road had been closed, but no one had told me. How could anyone have? I listened to tapes the whole way, so as not to be frightened by weather bulletins.

The sky was white, the highway was white, the entire world was white, except for the world within the confines of my little car. Only one lane in each direction was plowed, and it was almost impossible to discern the slightly darker white where the pavement showed through. The snow was falling too furiously for the road to be kept clear. Unfortunately, the exits hadn't been plowed, a problem I hadn't foreseen. Periodically, I saw half-buried cars in the drifts where others had tried to leave the highway. There were cars in ditches, or abandoned to the side, and a jackknifed tractor trailer. I was terrified, hurtling through the bleached-out wasteland, trying not to be mesmerized by the snowflakes bombarding my windshield. I knew that the landscape was not as soft as it appeared. Knuckles white, I clutched the steering wheel, clenched my teeth, and put my trust in front-wheel drive.

Maybe it was because I seemed to be inside a protective cocoon, or maybe it was because there was such a solid demarcation between inside and outside, or maybe it was some kind of chemical imbalance, but I began to feel very safe, still scared enough not to be stupid, but almost invincible. And I felt very strongly that it was because Paul was in the car with me, looking out for me. I talked to him, thanked him, tried to convince him to stay.

Afterwards, when I was safely home, I decided that it was true because I wanted so dearly for it to be so. There are those who would say he was there. But I think, if that were so, then why hasn't he been around all those other miserable, desperate times when I've needed him just as much, when I've sobbed his name aloud, begging for some sort of sign. I'd rather believe that he was there that day because I needed strength from deep within, where Paul is, because all that I loved in him is now mine, if I choose to accept that version of reality. Years passed before I could see through the pain to the gifts he had left me.

I have always held on to the last light at the end of the day, cherishing the time when color slowly drains out of the world, leaving only the countless variations of black and gray. When I am home, reading in the late afternoon, I wait until I can barely see before turning on a light. In movie parlance, the period between the setting of the sun and darkness is known as the "magic hour," when the sky is brightest, even though the light source is no longer visible. It is honored for its beauty. Schedules revolve around magic-hour shots. Everything must be ready, for this time doesn't last long, so there is a mad rush to take advantage of this special glow, this specific light. I lean against the cold, hard rock of the cliff until I can no longer see to write in the notebook on my lap. My eyes have adjusted gradually to the gloom and though anyone looking out from the security of a lit house might think it dark, I know better.

When night has truly fallen, I return to my room, where I realize I have been seduced by the way teardrops feel rolling slowly down my cheeks. Crying is a new skill that is practiced over and over, in its myriad forms, in variations I never knew existed. The warm water wells up in my eyes, spilling over, sliding unhindered until caught on my lips, tasting of the sea. Or sometimes, if I have thrown myself on to the bed, or am trying to sleep, the wetness flows directly onto the pillowcase, dampness speading until that side of my face is soaked, seeping into my hair, chilling me as the warmth rapidly cools. At times the sobs become convulsive, gulping chokes that strangle me. In the hospital, and several times since then, I have made myself ill with crying, as a child will, and have raced retching to the bathroom.

I had thought I was familiar with the sea, that I had become accustomed to the taste of salt on my lips, searing my throat, but I didn't know that a day would come when I would think that all I am is saltwater, that I would drown in the tears that fill my eyes, my heart, my life. A friend wrote to me, in her condolence card, that after such a loss, one never stops crying, but that in time the spaces between tears grow longer.

Every morning I awaken reluctantly, looking forward to only one thing. It arrives on a tray, a pitcher of steaming, fragrant coffee, and a smaller one of frothy, comforting milk. I pour some scalding milk into the oversized cup, then coffee. I gulp it greedily; it tastes too good to savor at first, and I am burnt for my impatience. I barely taste the flaky croissant or the crusty bread, eating quickly until the sawdust catches in my throat, then wash it down with the heavenly café-au-lait, never leaving a drop.

Food holds no appeal for me. I have lost my sense of hunger, or perhaps it is that I still equate eating with the English Channel. It was a game with us—how much can Sally eat, back when the fat was necessary to retain heat, before I realized that nothing on this earth could keep me warm. It will be years before I taste ice cream again; it is too rich, too creamy, too reminiscent of that summer. And too cold.

I put on a bathing suit, T-shirt, and shorts, stuff everything else in a canvas bag and stroll down to the beach. I spread out my towel, read, or lie inert, feeling activity swirl around me. If I am still and allow life to flow on without me, I will, perhaps, find peace. But there are days when the opposite is true; if I rush around, filling the time with meaningless chores, then the quiet comes. When I swim back and forth across the bay, I am languorous, expending no more energy than I must. It is more like sleepwalking than like the swimming I had known before. I allow the saltwater to cradle me, and the waves to gently rock me, and when I am soothed, and drowsy, I lie down on my towel and rest under the blanket of sunshine, until for some reason I sit bolt upright, and find a new diversion, or swim some more.

I rise in the morning for the coffee, and make it through the day for the sunsets. They are heartbreakingly beautiful, they mark another twenty-four hours passed. Tonight the sun had been obscured by the clouds long before it set, but I felt it go under, an obvious dimming of what had been before, a dying. The fishermen came in from their rocks, gathered their gear, and headed for home. The horizon disappeared.

S E P T E M B E R   1 6 ,   1 9 9 0

I realize that I needed to come to France to distance myself from the nightmare that was, and is, my life. Someday, hopefully, time will put me at a remove from grief, but until then, space seems to be the only way out. The physical law of light most important in painting landscapes is that objects become lighter in value and less saturated in hue as they recede into the distance. That is, the color is bleached out, the intensity fades away, the farther one is from something. For instance, far-off mountains are pale, blending into the sky, whereas those nearby have the richness of the vibrant colors of nature. This rule has long been essential in how I observe scenery; now it informs how I view my life.

My college lighting-design professor gave us an assignment on our first day of class. Every night for the next week, we were told, watch the sunset with a sketch pad in hand. From the time the sun touched the horizon, in intervals of five minutes until it was dark, he instructed us to diagram the sky, see the different colors, name them, notice what happened where they overlapped. We learned to look at how colors changed in relation to each other, how a salmon cloud pops out from a cerulean sky, and what happens when the edges aren't distinct but smudged together. We learned how the color theory of light differed from that of pigment, how all the colors in a paint palette mix to muddy gray, while all the colors in the rainbow mix to white. It wasn't an exercise in painting or drawing, but in seeing color, in observing light, so as to be able to translate the ethereal beauty of the natural world into a theatrical medium.

Whenever I asked, Paul would patiently explain to me why the sky is blue. It was something I could never remember, never quite understand. I loved it that he knew and didn't mind repeating it for me. The basic principle is known as "scattering" —the random deflection of light rays by fine particles such as those found in the atmosphere. The process is complicated by reflection, interference, and diffraction. Shorter wavelengths are scattered the most strongly, and the shortest wavelengths are blue, hence the color of the sky. Scattering by larger particles produces white, as in snow, or fog, or clouds, which do not actually change color during a sunset. One's perception of their color changes as the sun falls and the rays grow longer, catching the moisture in a different light. But the particles are themselves inherently colorless, as is water. The fact that this clear liquid appears to be turquoise, or celadon, or indigo is not a property of the water but rather due to many causes, a characteristic of the light received by the eye. It's how one sees things that makes them what they are.

These principles had always interested me, and the fact that they still did lent reality to the unreal situation in which I found myself. I was somewhere I'd never been before, where people spoke a language I didn't fully understand, but the laws of color and light were constant, even if other natural laws had been broken. The young are not meant to die before the old, and this should be an absolute. When it is not, one finds oneself on a strange planet where the sky is an odd color, where the ground underfoot shifts and rolls, where beliefs no longer hold. It is like going mad.

Paul had been told as a child that it doesn't rain at sea; that was how sailors knew they were approaching land—when they saw rain. How many times did we look out at the ocean and watch the rain and wonder where he heard that, and why he believed it—until I pointed out that of course it rains out there, just think of all those paintings of ships tossed about on stormy waves. I remember this discussion as I watch another sunset that I cannot see for the clouds, as it rains at sea.

S E P T E M B E R   1 8 ,   1 9 9 0

Six weeks ago today was the last day we were both alive. Maybe that's why I can't stop crying today, as if six weeks is any different from six minutes, or six years. On days like today

I reduce my life to a series of short-term goals. Okay, just stay here on the rocks for an hour and a half. Okay, you can stay in your room for another hour and a half. You can lie on your bed but you're not allowed to think. You must stay longer than two hours at the beach. Swim as long as you can bear to, lie on the sand until you can't not think, then back to the water, or a walk. Every hour is nothing more than sixty minutes gotten through.

I was once told that the rule of thumb in training is that every day off means a week to make up for it—to get back in shape. I also heard—maybe I've confused the two—that for every hour one is under anesthesia, a week is required to recover from it. There must be some kind of formula into which I can factor the loss of Paul—for all that we put into our time together and for all that we received, it's going to take me that much longer to recover from his death. How long, I want to know, how long will this last? I need to know the exact number of days, or even an approximate guess, so that I can have a goal, anything that hints there may be an end.

[It is now 1995. The time has come when the number of years since Paul's death equals the number of years we had together. I realize that math and logic are inapplicable. The time, though comprised of an equivalent amount of days, is not symmetrical. The years of loss will always weigh heavier, but they will never prevail over the years we had together.]

I traveled to Bordeaux, where there was an English-language bookstore. I had always been concerned about being stuck in a hotel room in a foreign country with nothing to peruse but a telephone book. Reading French required far more presence of mind than I had.

I changed trains in Bayonne, wandering around in circles, eye on my watch, waiting for the connection. When I arrived in Bordeaux, I meandered some more, in and out of antiques stores, cathedrals, up and down narrow streets. Nothing distracted me. I was too aware of the fact that I was just marking time, waiting for the train back to what seemed, by now, like home. I bought a couple of paperback books for an outrageous sum of money, books that were dense enough to slow down my reading but light enough to get through without the burden of someone else's heartbreak.

It is the latest I'd been out in a long time. The train arrived back in St.-Jean-de-Luz at 9:30. The streets of the town are brightly lit and lively, but the path along the water up the hill to the hotel is quiet and deserted, the pounding of the surf, the wind rustling through leaves vaguely menacing. Yet I am totally calm, tired but unconcerned. The absence of worry brings forth a new round of tears; now that the worst has happened, I have nothing left to fear.

This need to tempt fate continued for a long time, beyond France, into the years that follow Paul's death. In New York, I walk in areas I have been warned against, carelessly take the subway at night, volunteer for dangerous jobs at work, except those that involve painting near traffic. Two and a half years after Paul died, I worked all night during filming in an elegant apartment on the Upper East Side. I watched from the picture windows as the subtle illumination of dawn shimmered on the reservoir in Central Park, heard the welcome cry of "Wrap!" and decided that, instead of taking a cab, I would walk across the park and take the subway. It was early morning in early spring; the light was beautiful. The sun would not rise for some time. Along the eastern horizon the buildings were backlit in crimson as deep blue glowed above me; in the park there was still no color, only the contrasts in darkness between the open field, the charcoal trees, and the deep, deep shadows. I refused to be concerned about what lurked in those shadows, defiantly reveled in the pleasure of my solitary stroll, challenged fate to take its best shot. I saw no one, until I exited on the far side, and safely rode the empty subway home, unscathed, untouched, perhaps even lucky.

I think I am beyond this self-destructive phase, but four years and eight months after Paul's death, I fell in love with the wrong man, someone who made certain I was considering sharing a life again, who talked of a future together as if it existed, and then disappeared suddenly, without saying goodbye, or writing, leaving only a message on the answering machine promising to call soon, from the new city where he would be living. He did not leave a phone number. Weeks of silence passed, then months, and so many of my perceptions were once again washed away. Perhaps I was not the expert judge of character I considered myself to be, perhaps I am doomed to a life of abrupt endings, perhaps all the time alone has left me vulnerable, unfit, unrealistic. But all along, in the back of my mind was the worry that I was blinded by the wonder of being in love again, that this man was too much of an unknown to elicit such strong feelings so quickly.

I asked a friend to check the obituaries for me. After all, my fears were grounded in experience, but by then I knew the search would be negative. I spent a long time thinking, and was able to detect the warning signs. In the midst of the relationship, I saw what I wanted to believe was real, accepted as truth what I should have known was fiction. The words of love had come too easily, the assurances were given too quickly. They had no weight behind them, no appreciation of depth or difficulty, and were, therefore, empty. I loved talking to this man, spent hours on the phone. He once told me that saltwater has the same proportion of salinity as tears, that people are mistaken when they fear to open their eyes when swimming in the sea. He asked me to teach him how to swim.

SEPTEMBER 21, 1990

"Better day than most. The sunset is incroyable. I brought a book and a notebook but can only watch. When the sunsets alone are enough to make you cry, why fight it? As I watch the waves crashing through my tears, I notice that even the rocks weep saltwater here."

This is an almost unedited, unelaborated-on diary entry, unlike the rest, which have been rewritten to fit my changing view of all that happened. I cannot pretend to know five years later, as I try to make sense of what I wrote then, why one day was better than another. I don't remember feeling, at any point in France, that life was getting any easier, but apparently it was. The rawness was wearing off, or being absorbed, the intensity was dimming with the setting sun. The mysterious and uniquely personal process of healing had begun. I was too close to see, but I recognized some days as less tearful than others. It was a start.

S E P T E M B E R   2 2 ,   1 9 9 0

The beach is filthy today. Debris dumped from some distant ship has drifted into the bay. There are two-by-fours and plastic bottles and general trash. I would hate to swim into something unexpected, so I don't think I'll swim. It's been a long time since I've been able *not* to swim. Actually, truthfully, I still agonize over it—should I, shouldn't I? If I had been swimming just there, I would have been fine, I could have avoided that floating thing, I would have seen to swim around that, etc. Fearful that I was about to run screaming from the beach, I walked away from the temptation of the water.

I feel that I cannot think clearly. Much else is muffled in

attempting to swathe my thoughts in cotton gauze. When I feel myself becoming distressed by something so stupid as whether or not to swim, a curtain comes flying in, automatically, right on cue, stifling anything that might agitate. I fear that I shall cut myself off from memory, and feeling, and become a robot. Not a very smart one. Paul, when I would analyze something to death, would ask, "Can't you just stop thinking?"

"No," I would respond. "Can you? When you're not actually doing something, is your mind blank?" He replied that it was, but I didn't believe him. Even now, in trying so hard not to think, I need to be reading, or watching, or daydreaming in a tightly controlled way. Unbidden thoughts make me cry, so I leave them no room.

There is a tiny antiques store on one of the steep, narrow roads, where old linens are sold. Tables are piled high with starched, embroidered sheets, dresser drawers overflow with frothy lace, stiff brocade tablecloths droop in elegant curves. Almost everything is in shades of cream or ecru or crisply starched white, except for the odd pair of dove-gray gloves, or a black straw hat. There is a display case of heavy old jewelry, but mostly the place is brimming with fabric. For some inexplicable reason, I have decided that I want to bring home a souvenir from St.-Jean-de-Luz. Why I should ever want to remember this journey is beyond me. I had seen a small wooden religious statue in another antiques store but had been too intimidated to ask the price.

This was my second visit to the linen store and I was eager to find something. I searched through the lace-edged pillow-cases, remembering an unused pair we had received as a wedding gift, which I had been saving, for a special occasion, I guess. I examined delicate handkerchiefs, thinking nothing could be more appropriate, but pass them by, knowing they would just sit in a drawer at home. I had almost given up when I saw something resting on the floor, almost hidden in the folds of a damask tablecloth. A thin iron rod formed a frame, about eighteen inches square. Sewn to it was a piece of burlap from which lace had been crafted with sturdy linen string. The pattern was complex, a combination of open spaces where the burlap threads had been pulled and intricate designs where the linen had been woven into swirls of rosettes embellished with tiny knots. As I lifted it to look more closely, the woman whose store it was came over. She unpinned it and I recognized the shape as a curtain valance, meant either to border the top of a window or to diffuse the light coming through a small opening. The woman explained that the piece was in three parts, that the middle section was complete, the far left unstarted, except for the bottom edge, and the section in the frame had been in the process of being made when, for some reason, work had stopped: See, she pointed out, how the needle pierces the burlap where an unknown woman in another century placed it when she was interrupted. I look from the center section to the one to the right and realize that the pattern is not exactly the same. Although the piece in progress was visually symmetrical, there was no way of knowing how it would have ended, but even unfinished, it was beautiful.

When I returned to my hotel room, I realized that the frame was too large to fit into my suitcase. I didn't want to carry it in the paper bag; with my carry-on bag, I would not have had a free hand, a stupid way to travel. I walked back into town, to a store I had seen that sold fabric woven in the village. I bought a meter or so, some webbing, a needle and thread, and returned once more to my room. Curled up in the corner of my bed, windows open to a fresh breeze off the ocean, I sat sewing a bag with a shoulder strap. Suddenly I heard a kind of gasp, then saw two hands appear on the windowsill. "Hello?" I called out, startled enough to speak English, but frozen in place. "Pardon," I heard a man's voice say in French. The hands disappeared, followed by a thud as he dropped to the ground. I immediately looked in the spot where I had hidden my small suede bag of valuables. It was still there. I couldn't bear the thought of losing Paul's wedding ring. After I stopped shaking, I was amused, thinking that, as burglars go, he was at least polite. The hotel staff seemed only mildly concerned: after all, nothing had been taken. And for myself, I had long known that these things could happen anywhere, not just in New York.

S E P T E M B E R 2 3 , 1 9 9 0

Dreary, cold, wet Sunday. I feel as if nothing in my life will ever finish the way I'd like it to. I had hoped for one last swim here to end my stay, but I don't think it's going to be. One final walk along the cliffs probably won't happen either, just as one last goodbye never did. They sell a T-shirt in one of the stores—*carpe diem*, it says. I cringe whenever I see it. With rain cascading down the windows, what is there in this day that deserves to be seized, I wonder bitterly. Let me throw this day onto the garbage heap where it belongs, it means nothing to me, I only wait for it to be over and done with. I exist separately from this day, from this place, from myself. I reassure myself that as long as I can cope with simple daily chores, I surely must still be sane. Feeling cooped up by the rain, sick of being alone in a room with myself, I am still reluctant to walk outside, so I pace, sit, stand, stare out the window, pace.

Swimming in the rain is not necessarily unpleasant, but although I have been caught in many a downpour, I never willingly enter the water when it is raining, except for a race, or a scheduled event. I am embarrassed those times when I have been caught in the rain, chagrined that I read the sky wrong. One summer afternoon in Paradox, when Paul's father was visiting us, I escaped from the house to swim, asking Paul to start dinner while I was gone. It was late enough in the day that I couldn't tell if the clouds were darkening to let loose or if somewhere the sun was setting. Before jumping in, I covered my backpack with a plastic garbage bag, just in case. Somewhere between the nearest island and the dock, the sky burst. Rain shot straight down, blasting holes in the water surface, stinging my back. I stopped swimming to watch, opened my mouth to drink what I caught, barely able to see through the spray kicked up by the water pellets. There was no thunder, no lightning, nothing to detract from the wonder. I swam back and forth to the island a few times, treading water every so often just to look, and enjoy, until the rain let up and I climbed out.

When I arrived home, my wonderful mood was shattered. Paul and his father were sitting around, dinner not started. Annoyed, I began to say something, but Paul wouldn't let me, leading me upstairs to show me a surprise. In my absence, he and his father had wired some scavenged iron wall sconces and hung them on either side of the bed. They emitted a warm, soft glow in the drizzly evening. Even then I regretted my petulance; now I rue every unjustified bad mood, every word spoken in anger.

S E P T E M B E R   2 7 ,   1 9 9 0

Leafing through the mail waiting for me in New York, I find a letter from the Regional Transplant Program. "Paul's right kidney was successfully transplanted into a twenty-four-year-old man from the New York area. His left kidney was also successfully transplanted. The recipient was a thirty-four-year-old woman who is married and has two children. Paul's heart was successfully transplanted into a fifty-two-year-old man. His liver went to a forty-one-year-old woman from the New York area. All the recipients are doing very well at this time." The letter writer was effusive in his gratitude, thanking me for my generosity, and that of my husband, in giving others a new chance at life. I don't know if the letter was written by the man at the hospital or a stranger, but he referred to Paul's death as tragic and senseless, making the condolences he offered sound sincere and heartfelt.

Paul's thirty-fourth birthday. When Paul was a child, his birthday was celebrated on September 28. One day he started his first job, a paper route. He needed his birth certificate to obtain a social-security card and was surprised to discover that his date of birth was actually September 29. When he confronted his parents about the discrepancy, they just shrugged and figured that close was good enough. So, all his life, Paul had to stop and think to remember when his birthday really was. I had decided to buy him a chain saw this year, since I knew he wanted one. To think I was worried that he might hurt himself with it.

Because Paul never took to New York as I did, I felt a responsibility to try to make it fun for him, to show him all the possibilities. One year on his birthday, we both skipped work and drove out to Long Island in the early-morning twilight. As the sun rose, we boarded a fishing boat, one of those silly charters that are perfect because they're good at finding the fish, and they cleaned what we caught, and put us back on land by noon. We had lunch somewhere that I've long forgotten, then walked along a deserted Jones Beach, heads ducking into the wind, eyes down to keep the sand away from our contact lenses. I have a snapshot of Paul from this day framed on my dresser, with his leather jacket zipped all the way up, its collar pulled high to his chin, looking truly handsome.

I had snuck his birthday present into the apartment the night before. He closed his eyes, as instructed, while I put the roll of canvas in the back of the closet, pulling the coats together to hide it, extracting his solemn promise not to peek. When we arrived home that afternoon, I again wouldn't let him look and moved the canvas into his bedroom. I then mixed a batch of wallpaper paste while he pretended not to be curious. I wasn't pleased with the painting; I'm never satisfied with my work, even after years of Paul's reassurances. I glued it directly to the wall, then told him he could enter. He seemed to like it, a view of the Rockies as seen through the frame of a painted window, to remind him of the Colorado of his youth, to placate him while he put up with New York for my sake.

One year, I bought Paul a turtle for his birthday. For some reason, we had wandered through a few pet stores and he had been fascinated by the turtles. We both would have preferred a dog, but thought it unfair to coop one up in a New York City apartment. I rode home on the bus, with the bag holding the turtle inside the small aquarium resting on my lap. Paul wasn't there yet, so I hid the aquarium, now half filled with water and the turtle, behind the desk. I was going to wait until the next day, Paul's birthday, to give it to him, but I started worrying, what if I was doing something wrong, what if the turtle was dead in the morning, etc., so I presented it to him that night. Paul was thrilled, enchanted by the funny-looking but charming reptile. I thought it advantageous to encourage his affection for aquatic creatures. Because it was a gift for Paul, I let him choose its name, Tom. We were fairly sure it was a male.

After a while, Paul started thinking Tom was lonely, that he was swimming around the tank all day seeking companionship. So the next year on his birthday I brought home another turtle, probably a female, but this time I decided her name was Melanie, without giving Paul a chance to decide otherwise. Tom and Melanie never really established much rapport; indeed, they seemed to dislike each other. Melanie tended to stay on the bottom all day. She was a sort of turtle that had the ability to absorb oxygen from the water, through her skin, so she didn't need to come up for air very often. Tom was the swimmer—not very graceful perhaps, but speedier than one might think. We bought them a bigger tank. Sometimes Paul would pull his chair right up to the aquarium, lean his head on his hand, and watch Tom swim. I was fascinated by how Tom controlled his depth. He floated on the surface with outstretched arms and legs, then expelled air in gurgling bubbles when he was startled, so as to sink quickly to the bottom in order to hide.

We brought the turtles rocks from our travels, water-worn, colorful stones from the beach at Shelter Island where Paul's publisher was, a piece of roofing slate found in the sand at the base of Mont-Saint-Michel. I often find smooth, cool pebbles in jacket pockets that I meant to drop into the water but forgot about. As responsible adults, we learned as much as we could, or at least needed to, about turtles, and found that they could live as long or longer than people. Paul joked that we would have to decide who to leave them to in our wills.

Melanie died two years after Paul. She is buried, wrapped in a washcloth, in the garden, near Paul's ashes. I felt like a child, gravely laying a pet to rest, before remembering where exactly I was.

I bought Tom an even bigger aquarium. Sometimes my fierce affection for him alarms me; he is, after all, just a turtle, with a brain smaller than a pea, but he is also a living part of that other life. "Buy a dog," friends say, concerned about the time I spend alone. But I don't want to rely on the companionship of a pet, and I fear a dog would be intrusive, too living, too breathing.

This year of Paul's death, his birthday has fallen on Yom Yippur, the holiest day of the Jewish calendar, the Day of Atonement. Late in the afternoon, there is always a memorial service for those who died the previous year. I went with my parents to their temple in Pittsburgh, to hear Paul's name read. The words of the service were empty, the sermon meaningless, but the list of names—each one hit me. Most of the names were old-fashioned, surely elderly people, but I recognized the residue of sorrow behind each one. To hear Paul's name announced in so public a venue was a shock. I felt isolated, even in the company of mourners, even though the muffled sobs came from all directions.

I have not set foot in a temple since. For me, the answers lie elsewhere. But I have always been intrigued by the rituals of religion, and persist in fasting for Yom Kippur, or abstaining from leavened bread for Passover. While on a springtime visit to Italy three years later, Heather and I visited extraordinary cathedrals, with murals by Piero della Francesca and Domenico Ghirlandaio, paintings that I had known and loved in books, and had copied on walls of my house. Seeing them in all their glory moved me to tears, especially as the ravages of age, the missing chips, the water stains, were so evident. In every church, she and

I lit candles, for her husband, Rick, who was Catholic, and for Paul, who was not. The symbolism of the flickering flame transcended religion, rekindled our memories, became a ritual in which we saw both sorrow and humor.

S E P T E M B E R   3 0 ,   1 9 9 0

There is a 10K race and the finish line is beneath the windows of my parents' apartment. The first to cross are several men in wheelchairs. All I can think is, how lucky they are. Why can't I have Paul in a wheelchair or with a cane or with some sort of brain damage? Why can't I care for him and nurse him back to the best he can be, considering his injuries? Why can't I have him in sickness, if not in health, for worse if not for better, instead of not at all? All my hospital fantasies return, how I would be at his side for all the therapy, to help him learn to walk again, or adjust to a new life with limitations.

Once he woke up unable to move his neck, on a Saturday morning. It had happened before in his life, before he met me. He lay in bed, wincing and groaning, while I thumbed through the yellow pages, trying to find a chiropractor with Saturday office hours. One in the Village said to bring Paul in, he could make time for him. As I helped Paul dress, he gushed over me for taking care of him, which was silly, because I loved doing it, and surely we were beyond the stage where he should have felt he had to say thank-you. When the roles were reversed, I understood. When I tried to thank him for brewing a cup of tea or heating apple cider to soothe my frequent sore throats, he shushed me, telling me it was better not to talk, to rest my voice.

I live for the mail, for the condolence cards that continue to trickle in. I weep as I read the letters, but I hate days without them. My favorite cards are the ones that would appear to be inept—the woman who reminded me who she was by saying she swam in the next lane, the man who simply signed a standard card with "Hope to see you in the pool soon." They came from all religions; Paul has trees planted in his name in Israel, Masses were said, people who still believed in prayer prayed for him, and for me. His college roommate wrote of a Halloween party for which Paul helped with the decorations by filling the house with autumn leaves, and how years later they continued to find scraps of red and orange underneath furniture, in closet corners. Friends whose own tragedies I know don't tell me of their grief, but I feel the rush of kinship. Heather, whom I had barely met, sent a letter offering to talk when I was ready. She knew it would take time; she relived the horror of her loss when she heard of mine. Stories are recounted of siblings and parents and boyfriends, and children lost.

An older man who lives down the hall stopped me one day as I was entering our apartment with a basket of clean laundry. "I'm sorry. I wasn't going to say anything, but I have to. I heard about your husband. I needed to tell you that I am so sorry. My son died when he was your husband's age, leaving a wife and three children. I am so sorry for you"—tears in his eyes, running down my face. Since then, we chat whenever we see each other. He gives me advice, tells me not to compare when I start dating, says he loves me like a daughter, tenderly touches my face. I don't even know his name.

The days would seem to have a familiar routine: I wake up, I brew a cup of coffee, I wash my face, I brush my teeth. The only variation is that sometimes it is 7 a.m. when I finish, sometimes it is 3 p.m., and either way, it feels as if the same amount of time has elapsed and the same amount of time looms ahead. I catch myself watching the clock, to reassure myself that the minute hand must be moving if the second hand is.

I have eaten barely anything for two months, but I grow heavier and heavier. There are days when I don't have the strength to lift my legs, or the will to pull myself out of bed, hours spent waiting for the caffeine to kick in, trying to muster the energy to heat the water for another cup, as if a gallon of coffee would jolt me out of my lethargy. I know I should do something but can't think what. I do nothing but read mysteries, curled up in my corner of the sofa. In these books, death is nothing more than a plot device. No one mourns the departed; murder is a puzzle to be figured out. By the end of the story, it makes sense, there was a reason for it, if not for the victim, then for someone else. Loose ends are neatly tied up; friends, relatives, and detectives get on with their lives. There is rarely so much as a hint of the devastation left behind. For some reason, this appeals to me, this fiction of life lived after sudden death.

I'll need to leave town again soon. New York is dangerous, too many ghosts, too many places to avoid. I bravely venture into the world beyond my locked door only to have the breath knocked out of me by thinking I caught a glimpse of Paul in the crowd. This happened to me on Twenty-third Street, two blocks from where he died, in the middle of the afternoon. So many people on the sidewalk and just one who stopped me cold. He continued to approach until I forced myself to look away, summoning all my strength to remain standing.

I am beginning once again to feel the need to swim, but I am unable to go back to the health club where we swam together. Paul knew how it was, when we were on vacation somewhere, and I started acting a little cranky; all he had to do was get me to a pool. A human being can survive no longer than three days without water. Maybe this doesn't mean chlorinated water, or saltwater, but in my case it might as well.

When Paul and I first started dating, he was annoyed when I told friends who asked, no, he doesn't swim. "I do swim," he insisted. "Just because I don't swim like you doesn't mean I don't swim."

"If you can't swim more than a length without gasping for air, it doesn't count," I ruled. He gave in and let himself be taught how to breathe correctly, how to swim without lifting his head above the water. One day, in a very small pool, he challenged me to a race. As I knew would happen eventually, he beat me. It was humiliating, but I've learned that most men, because they are stronger, can beat me in a sprint, no matter how sloppy their stroke. Brute force counts for something in a short race. Paul was overjoyed. I continued to swim, and when he was rested, he challenged me again. And he won again. A few weeks later, he challenged me at our regular twenty-five-yard pool. I had a little more on the line there. A friend offered to judge—he was laughing so hard at the end I don't know why I believed him, but he insisted that Paul had won. Paul was so excited it was as if he had just won Olympic gold. He refused my challenge of a longer race.

Every so often I had tried to lift weights to increase my strength, but found it too boring, so I let myself quit, figuring that since there was only so much time I could reasonably spend training, it was silly to waste it on anything I didn't enjoy, that the hours would be put to better use by swimming. It's difficult to remember that there was once a time in my life when there were too many projects, too much to do, when twenty-four hours weren't enough.

O C T O B E R   1 1 ,   1 9 9 0

Paradox. Rain. I'm burning the logs that Paul carted in to keep warm. As the pile diminishes, I lose a little more. I want to save his wood, leave that neat stack as a memorial, but it's too cold not to have a fire going and there's nowhere else to store the logs. He had greatly expanded the woodpile that was inside. It made more sense to him to bring in many loads, and have it last several days, than to bring in a few pieces several times a day, as I had done B.P.

This was part of what I thought of as the Boy Scout side of Paul, this methodical, levelheaded way of doing things, but this characteristic went beyond logic, to whimsy. Sometimes when I swam, while he waited on the shore, he would build little mud dams for streams flowing into the lake, to see how long they would last before washing away. Or finding water trapped in a puddle, he would dig an escape trench for it, helping it find its way downhill. Or in the winter, upstate, in the places where the water went under the road, he would drop ice in one side, then run to the other side to wait for it to appear. He was fascinated by how things worked, by cause and effect. One evening, I was standing in the kitchen drinking beer from the bottle when Paul ever so gently pulled the bottle away from my lips. In the instant before I could turn the bottle upright, beer splashed down the front of my shirt. "Why did you do that," I asked, amazed. "What on earth possessed you?"

"Sorry. I just wanted to see what would happen."

I wander up and down the dirt roads of Paradox. The sunlight blazes through the fiery leaves; the ground glows with fallen color. One year, we took the canoe to Crane Pond on such a day. After paddling around exploring the shoreline, we stood at the water's edge, trying to take it all in, examining the shallow water in its intricate depth. The sandy bottom was clearly visible, littered with faded, long-dead leaves. We saw this filtered by the water itself, as through the slightly tinted glass of a paperweight. Vivid leaves, newly dead, floated on the surface, which acted as a window through which we looked inside, even as it reflected the clouds sailing through the sky above. "Could you paint that?" Paul asked.

"Of course," I said. "It would probably just take a really, really long time." So he challenged me to do it, trying always to prod me into reaching as far as I could. I said I would paint our bedroom floor just like that. The year after he died, I covered it with a sisal rug, instead.

The hint of winter waiting just beyond chills me, ruining autumn. I know what is coming, and that it will be too cold. To the north and the west there are no houses, so those are the directions I head. There is one stretch of road, cutting north through the valley, that before, when I was young, I especially loved. Something about the dilapidated red barns, the stream meandering through the field, the backdrop of mountains, stirred me. I remember thinking, back then, that no matter what, no matter how blue I was, this view would always lift my spirits. It does nothing for me now.

There is another run of dirt road, between our house and the paved street, that plunges bravely through marshland, barely higher than the water on either side. It floods every spring, and one year the beavers started to build a dam right down the middle of it, mistaking it for a shallow stream. On the eastern side is a tiny pond hidden in the weeds. In the spring the turtles bask on a half-submerged log, craning their necks toward the warmth of the sun. One summer, it was the favored feeding spot for a great blue heron. We watched it as we slowly drove by, trying not to disturb it, fascinated. Automatically, trip after trip, our heads turned, hoping to catch a glimpse of this magical bird. It was easy to mistake it for a dead tree limb, the gray of its feathers almost the color of driftwood, its long legs appearing like branches through the reeds. The difficulty in seeing it made it that much more special when we did.

Then one day, months later, in the middle of winter, probably on the way in to spend Christmas, I inadvertently, ever so slightly, turned my head to look as we passed the spot in the road. "Do you expect to see him with his feet stuck in the ice?" Paul teased me. In that moment, I was deeply moved by all we shared, by how well this man knew me, and that he loved me anyway.

A year or more after Paul died, I had a dream about the heron. I was looking out the window at a cloudy, ashen, El Greco sky when a heron flew into sight, sweeping across the field, growing larger and larger as it headed straight toward the house. I was terrified, struggling to wake up, to escape. The whoosh, whoosh of its wings was an ominous sound in the heavy silence. Just as it looked as if it would crash into the house, it soared overhead, floating out of my sight, leaving behind peace, and sleep, and, when I awoke, bafflement at why I had been frightened by something I loved so well.

Sitting in the warm kitchen of Judy and Martin's farmhouse, I wonder, I don't know what I'm supposed to do. Should I keep on wearing my wedding band? I see the pain in Judy's eyes.

"I don't think you have to worry about that now," she advises. And I don't. I wear it as long as it comforts, for several years, until it reproaches me for moving on, for wanting to meet someone, and for not wanting this fictitious man to think I am wed to another.

My wedding band had started to fall apart long before Paul died. It was a delicate ring set with tiny diamonds and my work was too rough on it. I wanted to get a simpler, stronger ring for everyday wear, but Paul had objected. "This is the ring with which I thee wed. How can you think of wearing a substitute ring?"

"But the ring is just a symbol," I countered. I had once mentioned the idea of dyeing my wedding dress so I could wear it again. Paul protested that as well. Now these tangible things mean so much to me I wonder how I could ever have taken them lightly. The things, of course, not what they represented. I hold Paul's wedding band in my hand for comfort, feel the weight of the pocket watch I gave him on our wedding day. It is antique; I wonder what happened to the man who owned it before Paul, did he leave a widow who sold his watch? The morning of our wedding was the only time I saw Paul cry. In our five years, the only tears, those of joy. How could his life have been so different from mine, when we shared so much? Surely he is the lucky one.

NOVEMBER 6, 1990

Election Day. I leave town so I won't have to vote. When I first started going out with Paul and told my friends about him, they tended to ask the same basic questions: does he swim (no), is he Jewish (no), and, to some of them I'd admit, but it gets worse, he's a Republican. They were horrified, as was I. Most of our worst arguments were political, and they did not end in laughter, but in oaths punctuated by slammed doors. I clearly remember thinking that I didn't see how I could make it through another Presidential election with this man. Obviously, I wasn't thinking clearly. I hadn't really meant it. We never converted each other, but we did come to respect each other's point of view every so often. I learned that Republicans weren't all mean-spirited, selfish people. I don't know what he learned about Democrats. In a way, though, I truly admired his perverse stand. I've always respected those who hold true to their opinions, no matter how unpopular, and being a Republican in New York City was definitely a lonely, uphill battle. But elections were difficult, because I knew that my vote was canceled out by the person closest to me in the world, and this saddened me.

So now that I had a chance to make my vote count, it was too painful to bear, the elections involved not worth it. That last night in the hospital, one of the deals I made with Paul was that, if he lived, I would vote Republican. I was willing to sell my soul, but since no one bought, I was free once again to cast my ballot as I chose. I chose not to. I drove to Cape Cod. It was actually a tremendous lift, to be driving down the highway with the windows open and country music on the radio, to be heading somewhere without painful memories. I had spent several months there in my college years, designing lights and painting scenery for a summer-stock company. Most of my time was spent confined in a high-school auditorium/theatre, but I never forgot how stunningly beautiful the Cape was.

After driving to the end of Cape Cod, I decided that Provincetown was far too lively, too populated, even at this time of the year, and I couldn't find a place to stay on the water. I traveled back down, stopping one night in a motel, the next in a bed-and-breakfast, where I spent my morning meal terrified that the host, who was moving from guest to guest, asking where they were from, what brought them to the Cape so late in the season, and so on, would find his way to my table. I gulped my coffee, swallowed my toast, and fled.

I searched the rentals in the local newspaper and found a backyard windmill in Chatham, which I rented for several weeks. Downstairs there was a living room and kitchen, up the spiral staircase, a bedroom. I could see a pond from my window, but not the sea, which lay just beyond. I walked to town each morning for my newspaper, the road bordered by hydrangeas still in bloom, returning me to France, providing my mourning with a state flower. I cut and dried a bunch to bring back to New York. The color didn't last, aging into the tea-stained ivory of old linen.

Somewhere along the way I picked up an old issue of *Cape Cod* magazine and came across an odd, strongly appealing painting. It was of a nun standing before a brick wall, which was only recognizable by the shape and texture of the bricks, as they were covered by a painting of sailboats floating on water. The nun was dressed in a medieval habit, including a butterfly hennin, a white starched-linen confection of a headdress. My scene-design professor in college said he could always tell what kind of day mine had been by how wrinkled the skin on my fingers was (the pool was two blocks from the theatre department). He also had a slew of aphorisms he dragged out at the drop of a hat: Never assume anything, presentation is everything, anything is possible, etc. My personal favorite was: "Life is a butterfly hennin." Finding this obscure reminder of times long gone touched me, as did the painting. The gallery that was using it as an advertisement was nearby, but closed for the season.

On a hunch, I looked up the artist's name in the phone book and found he was local, so I called. He told me he thought that particular painting had been sold but that a New York gallery handled his work, and a month later I went there. I fell in love with another painting of his—same nun, same butterfly hennin. She is standing in front of another brick wall on which is painted a Monet waterscape of Venice. The painting seems to be laden with symbolism. I don't know the artist's intention, but I know what it means to me, the memories that flood over me as I look at it, the personal resonance. The Monet is set in the night, lit by a streak of moonlight down the center of the water. In impressionistic silhouette is a shadowy gondolier standing at the stern, guiding his empty boat straight ahead through the light into the darkness. There is no one swimming at his side. Sometimes I think the nun has her head bowed, her back to the wall; sometimes I think she is facing it, looking up longingly. I prefer not knowing which. It was very expensive, but it had more meaning for me than money, so when I received the check for Paul's life insurance, I bought it. And sometimes, years later, when I look closely, I think I see a shadowy couple in the boat, lovers with their heads close together.

I have my bicycle with me and I ride to some beaches, drive to others, exploring as many as I can. When I arrive, I walk the length of the beach, struggling against the wind. I have beautiful photographs of sand and sea lit by glorious sunsets. Between France and the Cape I used up half a dozen rolls of film, with not a single person in a solitary picture. I don't fully understand my need to be near the ocean. Once it was because of the desire to swim, but the sea no longer draws me in, is no longer my intimate. I have become a spectator, observing from the shore, at a respectful remove from the stinging spray, lost in the simple beauty of light on water, mesmerized by the repetitive motion of the waves. They no longer frighten me, now that I remain on the beach, fully clothed, but rather seem to hypnotize me into a state that approaches peace of mind. I stop and stare until the cold drives me to move.

At some point, as early on as France, I started to feel a certain redemption in natural beauty, an easing of the pain brought on by the wonder of the setting of the sun seen through a salty haze. Occasionally, there are other lone walkers, but rarely are there the smug couples that seem to populate the rest of the world. At this time of year perhaps this is the place to walk one's troubles away. Making headway against the wind is too difficult, requires too much concentration for it to be romantic. The beaches here lack the civilization of France. The towns are hidden away somewhere, the paths are paved with sand instead of asphalt. I cannot read or write on these beaches—the wind would rip the pages out of my hands—so I am spared the burden of thinking, although I brought Paul's typewriter with me, for the nights.

I have learned that in times like these it is up to each individual to chose his or her solace. Mine might have driven most mad, those solitary walks along deserted beaches, the telephone my closest connection to those I loved, but it worked for me. I was, at the time, without rational plan, without any knowledge of why I did what I did or went where I went, but with the sense that I was moving in the direction I needed to go. All the traveling was a way of buying time, of waiting until I was ready to continue. I was wrapping my memories in the diaphanous fog that veiled most of our swims, so that life with Paul became a barely remembered dream. As I talk to others who have known what this is like, I see that there is no one way, no tried-and-true system. The method suits the mourner. I will not judge anyone for the path they choose to follow. After all, nothing about any of this feels like a choice.

My Australian sister-in-law, Sue, was having dinner with her late husband's best friend and his wife on the first anniversary of John's death. She spoke of how lonely she felt, how she wished she would meet someone, so she could share her life in the wonderful way she had known before. The friend was shocked, thought it an insult to John's memory to be thinking such thoughts so, to him, soon. He couldn't begin to fathom how long a year could be or, more accurately, in Sue's life, two years—a year of dying followed by a year of grieving. Sitting there, with his wife at his side, he dared to judge her harshly.

I was appalled when she told me this story. It is one of the legacies of these Carter men we married that the companionship they gave us makes the solitude that much lonelier, the loss that much deeper. To want what we had before, even knowing what we know now, is a tribute, not a dishonor. I once told Sue that, had our positions been reversed, had it been me in that hospital instead of Paul, I would have wanted him to fall in love with one of the nurses caring for me, so that he wouldn't have had to know for five minutes the emptiness I have known these past years. Sue had thought of these things as well. She said that, had she been the one being wasted by cancer over the course of those long months, she would have been arranging dates for John, trying to find someone to be at his side when she died.

A woman I know who was widowed young, never having lived alone, took a lover shortly after her husband died. It didn't last; there was no way it could have. She's gone through many men since then, desperate to be married again, searching the personal ads, traveling the world to keep busy, always hoping, always trying so hard, ashamed of how she fears her husband would see her if he could. It makes me sad to watch her, but I also admire her for not giving up, for rising to her feet each time she is knocked down. We re-create our lives to adapt to the circumstances in ways that suit our natures, and we have learned not to judge the roads to peace that others follow. Just as we had no say about being widowed, or losing those we couldn't live without, we are limited in how we move beyond this, by circumstance, and personality.

At some of the Cape beaches, the tide goes out forever. Standing in a sandy parking lot at low tide, I could barely see the waves breaking off in the distance. One day I bought a pair of bright yellow rain boots and that evening I shuffled out to sea as far as I could, skirting the deeper water, sloshing through puddles, and still the actual surf was at a fair remove. It was becoming too dark, or I was too tired, or it was time to swim. I tried again the next evening. Once again, night fell while I was still far from my goal. I was sidetracked too often, exploring tidal pools, photographing intricate ripples in the sand, or a rock that glowed crimson in the sunset. I vowed to go back there someday and at low tide walk all the way to the edge of the ocean.

Most evenings, after watching the sunset, I swam at the YMCA in Hyannis. They told me that I would be allowed to use the pool only twice, on a day pass, before I had to join for an entire year. I figured that if I explained my situation someone would be compassionate enough to bend the rules, but I didn't want to explain, so instead I cheated and signed in under different names: my real name, Paul's name that I hadn't used when he was alive, my sister's married name. The people behind the desk changed frequently, and even when they didn't, no one remembered me. Maybe I really was invisible.

I don't understand why it is so often so difficult to work one's way into a swimming pool, any more than I know why so much of the shoreline should be private, making access to so many lakes so complicated. When I was a stage manager for dance companies on tour, I made it into a game—what would it take to get into the nicest pool in town? I always traveled with newspaper clippings, to prove that I knew what I was doing. There's something about strange pools that gives me butterflies, reminds me of swim meets I have suffered through, but also thrills me by making the familiar unusual. Even though almost all the pools were twenty-five yards long, each one feels different, as if I were swimming in a new body of water. I always have to adjust my first few flip turns, figure out whether there's a ladder to warn me of the impending wall when I'm doing the backstroke leg of an individual medley, work out the lane quirks, realize time after time that "fast lane" unfortunately means anything but.

My favorite illegal activity is to get into a pool by unauthorized means, without paying. Once I'm in the water, past the bureaucrats, no one stops me. The lifeguards are always nice; they recognize one of their own. In St.-Malo, France, I was invited to swim with the local team and then allowed to stay in the gorgeous fifty-meter pool, which looked out onto the English Channel, after it was closed to the public. In Glens Falls, New York, I was told that nonmembers weren't permitted to swim during the early-morning hours because there was no one on duty to check membership cards. I swam for free whenever I was in the area, until, one morning, there was suddenly someone at the front desk. While working in Princeton on a movie, I found that no one questioned me when I walked into the locker room of the university aquatic center, then into the pool. I thought I was caught one evening when the lifeguard came over to me, but she just asked if I would mind swimming a lane line across. In one Midwestern college pool many, many years ago, as I walked toward the locker room after my morning workout, the guard asked me was I training for the English Channel. In Hyannis, the local coach wanted to know where I *used* to swim. I tried not to be annoyed. I was, after all, out of shape, but I was remembering how good I feel after a swim, how much more comforting earned physical exhaustion is than that imposed by a sleeping pill.

Because the Cape is so much farther east but still in the same time zone as New York, or Ohio, for that matter, the sun sets way too early. It is November and it feels like the dead of night by 4:00. I think about renting a place for December but have misgivings about the extended hours of darkness, as I tend to be very light-oriented. I envied Paul for the way he could come home after a day's work, eat dinner, then go to the computer to work on his next book. At least, that's what I thought he was doing, until I caught him playing games a few times. One evening, that last summer, I remarked petulantly that I was starting to feel like a "book widow" again. He fussed and apologized for neglecting me and showered me with the attention I craved.

I spent most of December in New York, then Christmas week with my family in California, making sure to be back upstate for a solitary New Year's Eve. Cross-country skiing had become my winter replacement for swimming while in Paradox—the closest indoor pool was an hour's drive away. Paul preferred the thrill of downhill skiing, so more often than not, while I skied, he would play around in the woods, cutting down low-hanging branches, thinning out pine-tree seedlings. We spent one Christmas of our life together with his family in Colorado. It wasn't even ten years ago, but the subsequent twists of fate are more evocative of a Greek tragedy than of an American family. Paul's mother died the following year, then Paul two and a half years later, then his older brother in another two years; then my father-in-law, who could bear no more, killed himself six months later, the day before Christmas Eve, 1994, as those of us who were left were heading to Colorado for an already sorely diminished family reunion. The one divorce that occurred seems minor now, though it was not at all, for it involved a child, and an alcoholic.

But that first Christmas we enjoyed ourselves. Paul's nephews loved to talk about their crazy uncle, how he was a wild man on skis, careening down the most difficult slopes with more nerve than skill. I realized that this man I loved had, like all of us, settled down with age, and become more wary of risk. Paul's brother-in-law talked me into going to an intermediate slope, although I protested that the beginners' hill suited me fine. The ski area was on the Continental Divide and the ride up the lift was spectacular. When we skied over to the new slope, I knew it was more than I could handle, between the moguls and the steep angle. Paul tried to help me make my way down slowly, but I was too scared and started to cry. He reassured me, helped me remove my skis, then took off his and walked me down the mountain.

There's an old logging road that winds through the woods behind the house in Paradox; it's one of my favorite places to ski. This particular winter, a neighbor had told me that where the road was too overgrown, the stream beside it was frozen enough to ski safely on, that I could follow his tracks, since he had done it the week before. I left the house in late afternoon. It was one of those days when it took forever to get going. The sky was clouded in, the forecast was for snow. I made it to the stream, then skied tentatively in Michael's tracks. There was open water beside me, but I knew I weighed less than he did. I remembered a Christmas hike Paul and I had taken back there one year. He was walking out on the ice, despite my warnings, and sure enough, went through up to his knee with one leg. He was incredibly quick about scrambling out without getting any wetter, and then insisted that he was fine, that he wasn't cold at all, he didn't need to go back to the house for dry clothes. I really miss that male point of view, that anything was better than admitting stupidity. I glided past the spot, concentrating on where I was going, finally arriving at Ingall's Marsh, a wide-open flatland with splotches of ice and water outlined in dead brush. The ghosts of dead trees, their roots drowned when the beavers changed the landscape, reached blackened arms to the dusky sky. Wind rustled through desiccated reeds as leaves skittered across the snow.

I wanted to ski farther, but darkness was falling and there were no tracks to guide me, so I turned around. On the trip home, it snowed really hard. The world was entirely monochromatic, a rainbow of shades of gray, leaving no way of knowing that the balsams and firs were actually green, except for a sense memory of what they looked like in the light. Clumps of snow lay like highlights on pine boughs, and soft white lines traced the lacy patterns of bare branches. The air was ashen with snow, the sky glimmered silver, the trees were dark behind a translucent veil. It was so lovely and magical that I found myself feeling grateful to be there to see it. If only I could have shared my wonder at finding beauty in a world without color, I couldn't help but think. I was soaked when I arrived home, covered in snow, perfectly exhausted, pleasantly breathless.

I still hadn't gone back to work. Money was not a problem, what with all we had saved for the Channel, and Paul's accumulated vacation pay, and constant gifts from my generous parents. I had been scheduled to start work on a movie, *Billy Bathgate*, on what was supposed to be my triumphant return from England. I was offered the job again, after Paul died, and told that it would be all right if I needed to disappear into the ladies' room every so often to "blubber." But once I started crying, it was impossible to stop until that round of tears was spent, which often took a long time. "Pulling myself together" after a short bout of misery was beyond my capability. And I hated crying in public. A few years later, I don't mind so much. The tears can be controlled, reined in, and it no longer worries me, the fear that anyone might see. If couples can hold hands in plain view, not caring how it affects anyone else, I can weep.

Sleep continued to elude me. I stayed on my half of the bed, knowing that the open sea on the other side was treacherous. Reading late into the night, still mostly mysteries, feeling the building and the street sink into slumber around me, almost put me to sleep. But as tired as I was, as heavy as my eyelids were, more often than not, as soon as I turned out the light, I was wide awake. Lying in bed was dangerous, so I would sit back up, turn the light back on, and start reading again, quickly, before the memories flooded back, and the tears overflowed. I became familiar with a time of night I had never really known, until it became almost comfortable to me. I learned not to fight for sleep, to relish the feeling that I was the only one awake, different from those who slumbered around me. I was up most of the night most nights, until after a few days, exhausted, I took a sleeping pill and sank gratefully into oblivion. I was always tired the days after I slept, and tired the days after I didn't sleep. Movie work usually started at 7:00 or 7:30; theatre at 8:00, which meant setting the alarm for 5:00 or 5:30. I had barely fallen asleep by then.

Sleep deprivation affects the body much the way shock does, leaving a floating disorientation, a strange sense of movement at the periphery of awareness, even when there is nothing there. And the dreams. I wish I had written them down from the beginning, but even without notes, I'll never forget my early dreams; they were unvaried, constant. Paul was hurt, injured, in some kind of trouble, but alive, and I had to get to him, to save him, but I couldn't get there, no matter how hard I tried, however I struggled against whatever was holding me back. In the winter of 1992, when Don was dying, I visited him often, in several hospitals, and finally in his own apartment. Sometime in the midst of it all, toward the end, I dreamed that I had forgotten to ask him to give my love to Paul, and to tell him how much I missed him, something I had meant to do because I knew they would be seeing each other. When I awoke, I knew it was unnecesary, and unkind.

In January of 1993, I dreamed I had two telephone lines. I was in the bedroom talking on one when the phone in the living room rang. The answering machine picked up. It was Paul, leaving a message. He was saying that he had arrived at the airport and wanted me to come for him, but since I wasn't there, he'd find his own way in. (I often met his plane when he returned from business trips.) I tried to rid myself of the person chatting in my ear, so I could talk to Paul, to tell him I'd be there, but I couldn't. Just as I managed to get to the other phone, I heard the click of the receiver being hung up. The next month I dreamed that Paul was alive but I had just discovered it, after thinking him dead for so long. We made love. He asked me why I hadn't believed in him, had given up on him. I wondered how I was going to explain to everyone who thought he was dead that he wasn't. I never found a way to stay in that small window of time between awakening and remembering.

It's been a long time since I've dreamed of Paul. These days, when I have trouble falling asleep, I swim laps, the way others might count sheep. Mostly I imagine long, slow, graceful butterfly, until its rhythm lulls me to sleep.

I still had no appetite, could barely eat. My sister sent packages of treats from Los Angeles. I wished she wouldn't, because I just wanted to waste away, to disappear. I took pleasure in the empty space between the waistband on my jeans and my stomach, in the feeling that I was swimming in my clothes from before. It was important to know that I had changed physically, that no aspect of my life was untouched. My hair grew longer and longer; I wouldn't let anyone cut it. I trim it myself when I think of it.

Paul and I had bought a new sofa before we were married. Even though we were in our thirties, it was the first, and last, piece of real adult furniture we bought together. Everything else in our apartment seemed to be a cast-off from friends, treasures we found on New York streets, purchases from the Salvation Army. We always tried to keep our sofa clean, swore never to bring food or drink near it, not wanting spills to mar such an expensive purchase. For spite, I ate all my meals there, in my corner, and continue to do so. On those rare occasions when I have company, I turn the cushions upside down, so that the clean side shows and the dark, stained side is hidden.

I screened all my calls on the answering machine. Friends stopped calling. Time was going by without me. I had nothing to show for my waking hours. I lost track of "lost days," days that I spent staring out the window, walking through the park, counting minutes. One of Paul's ideas was to make an eight-day calendar. Between Sunday and Monday would be "Funday," and that would be the true holiday, not to be wasted on obligatory chores. I thought it was a stupid concept. "What good would it do to put an extra space on a calendar, to signify time that doesn't exist?" I asked.

"It would make people think about what they would do if the time were there, and maybe prioritize, so that they would find the time. It would make every week feel like it had a three-day weekend." No matter how he explained, I was too literal-minded to accept a day that wasn't real. Now it makes even less sense to me, when the weeks are already seven days too long.

I talked to my sister every day; sometimes those were the only words that left my lips. I was living in my head, but trying not to think. I didn't know if being alone intensified the grief; I knew that being among people did. I thought I liked solitude, but this was surely beyond anything I could grow to like. There just didn't seem to be a viable alternative. Widowhood felt like a physical affliction—just as a blind person knows that no seeing person can understand sightlessness, I had no interest in lives untouched by tragedy. Such lives are few and far between, but at the time I couldn't see that.

When I tried to talk to old friends I found that I no longer spoke their language, that simple conversations left too many scars. One friend complained that she hadn't slept well because her husband had arrived home late and awakened her and she couldn't fall back to sleep. Another friend was thrilled when her husband was out of town for a night and she finally had some time to herself. To this day, I cannot bear to listen to complaints about spouses, and then it was all I could do not to scream, to try to hurt them back, to say the cruelest thing that came to mind. It was easier not to return phone calls. My sister's sensitivity amazed me, as if she could intuit what to say, and what not to say. As far as I know, she and her husband have not fought in the five years since Paul's death, although this is surely impossible. She senses that these are things I do not need to hear, and her generosity in always thinking of me first overwhelms me.

A day without tears still seemed so far into the distant future as to be beyond contemplation. Paul's father, when we spoke, assured me that it was good to cry, not realizing that it was impossible not to. My parents wanted me to talk to someone, to see a therapist. For what, I thought, so I could cry for an hour, then hand over a hundred dollars? My mother called a psychiatrist, worried about my depression. He asked if I had been like this before Paul died. "Of course not," she said.

"Well," he replied, "it sounds like she's having a perfectly normal reaction to a devastating experience." I realize that my parents wanted to help me, wanted me to feel better, but that would mean somehow denying my experience. I sought a way out of the sorrow but no one could tell me how, I would have to learn for myself. I read of a study in *The New York Times* proving that writing was just as effective a means for solving psychological problems as talking. It was the figuring things out, putting words to the feelings that was the key. I found that I could write sentences down on paper, but could not speak them, and by the time I could talk, I found that widowed friends and my sister were all the listeners I wanted or needed.

All my life, or at least as long as I could remember, I had wanted to swim the English Channel and I had wanted to write a book. As a child, I would two-finger-type stories on the manual typewriter in the basement, tie them up in brown paper and string, just like Jo did in *Little Women*, and send them off to various fiction contests, never to be seen again. My father insisted that I take a typing class in high school, imagining that it would be of use when I was in law school. I am grateful that I relented on the issue of typing class, and that I didn't on the rest of it. After a few creative-writing classes in college, and several false starts on novels that never made it to short-story length, I concentrated on what I felt I needed to do to make a living. But I never stopped writing. Each time the effort ended after a few pages, I told myself I was just waiting for the right story to come along, thinking that would make the process easier.

Paul knew about these dreams, and he knew that they would never be any more than that without a little prodding, so he would give me assignments: character sketches of the neighbors, stories about my family. He convinced me to try to write about the English Channel for *The New Yorker*, not for some swimming magazine, and suggested the diary form. He couldn't have known how infinitely more painful choosing words would be than swimming seventy-two strokes a minute for a mere ten hours, or eleven, or a hundred. I had been lazy about it, had only written a page or two about the Montauk swim before he died. He was lenient, told me that was okay; after all, most of the story was supposed to take place in England, and France, and somewhere in between. At Paul's funeral, a few people said there had to be a purpose, some reason, and although I recoiled from such sentiment, I also latched onto it, determined to create my own meaning.

I hadn't been back to our health-club pool, and leaving town in order to work out was wearing thin. I was desperate for a swim. Brian offered to come along to keep me company. Before he arrived, I did the paperwork to reopen my membership. The manager officiously gave me a hard time for freezing it longer than the three months allowed. I told her I had received permission to keep my membership frozen as long as I needed. "Why?" she asked, disinterested, cold.

"Because my husband died," I blurted out, the words all but lost in the sob. Repentant, horrified, distressed, she apologized profusely.

Brian arrived. We swam. I could barely keep up, even though he tried to make it easy for me. An acquaintance from the pool, whose wedding took place the summer after ours, greeted me, "Hey, Sally! How was the English Channel? I can't believe I haven't seen you since then!"

I froze. I couldn't say the words twice in one evening. Instead, I said, "This is Brian. He's going to tell you what happened," and wandered away so I wouldn't have to listen. I have learned, whenever possible, when it doesn't matter, to take the easy way out.

I thought that if I could just make it through the holidays, I'd be okay. What I should have known was that it wasn't just this day that would be bad, or that day, but an endless succession of days, and that the worst ones had a way of sneaking up from behind. I could anesthetize myself through Christmas, but not through the rest of my life. After the first of the year, I thought, I'll really try to return to work. But then I needed to get past the aftermath. I understood the despair of those who wait until after the New Year to kill themselves. Holidays and birthdays and anniversaries were rough, but it was what I didn't see coming that felled me, the memories that assaulted me at odd times, punching me in the gut, forcing me to pull off the road, to hold it inside until I could make it to the closest subway station to get me home. The pain was no longer constant but rather ebbed and flowed. The variation made living possible. I knew that while the better times wouldn't last forever, neither would the bad. There were days when I thought I would be able to make it through this. Then, suddenly, at times without reason, there would come a day when it was once again too much to bear, when I was inundated with grief.

The smallest thing could shatter my fragile shell—a song on the radio, an offhand remark. One day at the pool, a woman I know remarked on how thin I was, how great I looked, what was my secret. I just shrugged, and withered a little. There was a woman in one of the antiques stores on Cape Cod who, when I entered the store in the middle of the week, in the middle of the off-season, asked, "What are you doing all the way out here alone?"

These people never knew how their simple words hurt. They strengthen my resolve to be careful about what I say to strangers, and what questions I ask. A friend whose brother died in a robbery while a young man told me how wrenching the innocuous question "Do you have any brothers or sisters?" could be. So my conversations are perhaps more circumspect than they need be. I would rather err on the side of respect for privacy, and private hurt, than unintentionally open a wound. And as for the people I barely know who look deep into my eyes and ask, "No. *Really*, how are you?" unwilling to settle for the okay I've just given them, I wished I could have said, "I barely know you. Why on earth would you think I'd suffer through pouring my heart out to a stranger?" Those I love are incredibly dear to me, but acquaintances and strangers would do just as well to keep their distance. There is something to be said for talking about the weather.

I knew I had to go back to work, if only to get out of the house, out of myself, and to keep my health benefits. I reluctantly surrendered to the urge to move on to the next phase of the process, the emergence from the shelter of my cave to the real world. Paul once told me about a hike he had taken when he was a teenager living in Boulder. Outside of town were some rock formations known as the Flatirons, so named because they resembled irons sitting upright on an ironing board, with one side totally vertical and the other not quite, but almost, as steep.

He and a buddy climbed to the top of one of them, on a whim, to see if they could do it. They hadn't thought quite far enough ahead, to how they were going to get down. It was the kind of descent that has to be done backwards, blindly, which is far scarier than scrambling up. So they spent the afternoon sitting on the summit, waiting. Nothing was going to change, the incline wasn't going to become less extreme, no one was going to rescue them, but they weren't about to climb down until they absolutely had to. Evening shadows were creeping up from the valley by the time they finally inched their way down, making it home safely in time for dinner, telling no one how scared they had been.

I had waited as long as I could. I called a friend and asked him to consider me the next time he needed an extra scenic artist. One day the phone rang. I arrived at work exhausted, then tried to pretend that the past six months hadn't existed. It was a chore to figure out who knew, who didn't. Obviously, the other scenic artists knew; most of the carpenters didn't. That first day back, one of the carpenters, someone I didn't remember ever seeing before, asked as I walked by, "Hey, did your husband go to the USITT convention?" The guys liked to be part of the in-crowd of those who knew that Paul had written *The Backstage Handbook*. I had always been flattered by this in the long-ago past.

"Uh, no," I stammered.

"Yeah, well, I heard it was pretty boring anyway." End of conversation.

Later that day, I asked the friend with whom I was working if he could do me the favor of telling the carpenter what had happened. I had yet to say the words and remain dry-eyed, and I refused to weep at work if I could help it. It made getting through the days that much more exhausting. The work of a scenic artist is very physical, but nothing compared to holding back tears for eight hours.

It was so strange to be back among people. Time had healed in that scar tissue had started to form, but it was unlike normal skin, and easily ripped asunder. The subway ride to work was my respite; among strangers, I could be myself. As I walked into the door of the studio, I put on my mask, tentatively smiled good morning, and responded to each "How are you?" with a strangled "Okay," which was not technically true, but they didn't want the truth, even were I willing to offer it. I changed from my street clothes into my paint clothes, one costume into another. I hadn't been wearing black long enough to have old jeans or shirts to turn into work clothes, and was forced to wear colors, clothing from before. Drinking coffee, we stood around. They chatted. I had lost the ability, so I listened, and watched, to know how to behave again. People weren't sure how to treat me, nor I them. Months later, when I could, I sometimes mentioned Paul to see them squirm, but also because I had become comfortable talking about him again, and did not care if they were not.

I did the same work as everybody else. It was so familiar but so different. I did not shirk the strenuous jobs. I offered to climb the scaffolding, used the highest ladder, carried the buckets of cement and paint across the shop. My weariness was no longer physical, although it lay deep in my bones. Troweling joint compound in circular sweeps across plywood, rolling heavy texture paint onto vast surfaces, caused my shoulders to ache, my neck to burn, but the weight started to feel as much like strength as burden. The activity was a new way to pass time. Before, I was waiting for the minutes to inch by, now I was rushing the hours along with every stroke of the brush. When my mind wandered as I squirted tinting color into paint, I just stirred more vigorously, concentrated on mixing the exact shade. Sometimes I swam after work, it was the same subway station for the pool as for the train home, but usually I was too anxious to return to the comfort of my cocoon. I deserved to take the easy path out. I was alive, and I was working. It was enough.

FEBRUARY 1991

I did my Manhattan record swim on Wednesday, September 7, 1983, seven hours of swimming as fast as I could, trying to beat the sunset, and the clock. On Thursday I couldn't lift my arms, my throat was raspy, I ached all over, made it through a day of work hoping no one would notice how little I accomplished. On Friday I showed up at the pool and swam not very far, not very fast. That afternoon I drove from New York to Maine to do a ten-mile swim scheduled for the next day. I was doing it as a favor for a friend from our Clemente Manta Ray Swim Team, to raise money for a cancer hospice, as a memorial for his sister, who had died the previous year. I had received all my pledges long before I knew about the Manhattan swim and felt obliged to make good on my promise.

I arrived at dusk at the house of my friend's parents, a cabin sheltered in the deep shadow of a heavily wooded lakefront. The mother opened the door for me. I hadn't really thought about what had happened until I saw the sorrow in her sunken eyes, the grief in her gaunt face, and I was hit full-force with how it must have been to nurse her child to her death, and how it would be to have me in her house, spending the night in her daughter's room, when I was so healthy and so close in age to that young woman. There was a wheelchair in the corner of the room I was given, the daughter's picture on the bureau, various belongings scattered in among the medical equipment. The raw tragedy of death was oppressive. I slept fitfully, haunted by her presence.

I wonder now if that would be how a stranger would see me seven months after Paul's death, how my apartment would appear, my face, my life. His toothbrush still shares the cup in the bathroom with mine, his glasses gather dust on the nightstand, the shoes he was wearing that day, with the socks tucked inside them, wait beside the bed. The time will surely come when I will remove these things, but for now to live without them would be upsetting; to see them every day, a bittersweet reminder. And five years later I realize that if anyone were to look closely at my apartment, they might think I'm crazy; although the toothbrush is gone, and the glasses have been put away, Paul's shirts still hang in the closet, and his hiking boots still sit under the desk, beside me as I write. It doesn't seem morbid to me, it doesn't feel like I'm stuck in the past, but it is part of whoever I am, and will always be. Paul will never leave my life, although his place in it changes. His old shoes could go at any time—at this point, perhaps, his things are still around because I am such a lackadaisical housekeeper. The jars of anhydrous lanolin that Paul was to bring to England for me remain on the closet shelf, but that is because I would like, someday, to do other long swims, the length of Lake George perhaps, and surely lanolin keeps forever.

Each small change begets another, setting in motion what sometimes feels like an uncontrollable chain reaction. For years our bedroom needed to be painted but I resisted, not wanting to erase the scuff mark Paul's bicycle seat had left where it leaned against the wall. I had long ago given his bicycle to my cousin. The painting of the Colorado mountains bothered me; there were too many brushstrokes I wanted to change, but I didn't want to work on it anymore. While visiting some scenic-artist friends, I saw a painting that one of them had done, of a foggy, windswept sea. In the clouds above loomed a frigate, a seabird known for its long-distance flights. The bird's wings are outstretched in, it appears to me, a gesture of comfort, or protection. The artist kindly sold me the painting for a day's pay, although I knew it took far longer than a day to paint it. With relief I pulled my landscape off the wall, rolled it onto a cardboard tube and hid it in the back of a closet. I felt forced to paint the bedroom to provide a fresh background for my new seascape, but I was content when I was done.

A friend whose lover died of AIDS once said, "I guess it's made me a more compassionate person, but I was already compassionate." It was after Paul died and I knew what he meant, but now my sympathy knows no bounds for those I consider to have suffered as I have. I search the obituaries for people who died young, read between the lines to learn how and envy those who die within weeks of their spouse, or at their side. I weep as I read the newspaper, about a child killed by a drunk driver, about a woman whose husband died in a climbing accident; about a young mother swept out to sea by a freak wave. I cry for those whose love was shattered in the horror of a split second, and pity those whose private sorrow comes under public inspection. I lose respect for any journalist who asks, stupidly, "How do you feel?" as if a sound bite would suffice, when volumes don't. And as I read, I am very aware of the fact that I am going about my daily activities as I imagine, and remember, what others are suffering at the same time. I am drawn to the hidden heartbreak of strangers, and I feel an unbreakable bond with friends who have suffered overwhelming loss.

My friend Manfred's son died in an accident while Paul was still alive. It was some years after I worked at the Parade studio, but I grieved for Manfred, and remembered how often he spoke of Glenn, so we went to the funeral home to pay a condolence call. I dreaded going. I had never been in a room with an open casket, never seen the body of a young man, and I tried not to look as the line of mourners moved slowly forward. Manfred saw me when there were still several people between us, and before I knew it, had his arms around me, weeping deeply as he tried to talk, to explain that after the accident Glenn was alive, that they spoke in his hospital room, that it shouldn't have happened, it must have been a mistake, he was supposed to survive. Like a child seeing an adult cry for the first time, I was at a loss, unequal to the intensity of his sorrow. All I could do was sob, and wish I had answers, or at least words, but all I could say, over and over, was, "I'm so sorry. I'm so sorry." And even now, when a friend asks me for advice about what to say, how to comfort someone, all I can think of is, "I'm so sorry," and "It shouldn't have happened." There are times when the words are utterly ineffectual. It is only after, later, in retrospect, that the kindness can be sorted out from the pain, that the condolences make any sense, that lessons can be gleaned from those who have gone before.

I try to stop by the Parade studio every so often. I see how Manfred has changed, and inquire after his wife and daughter. And he speaks truthfully, if sadly, knowing that with me, he needn't pretend that everything is fine. It is a relief to have friends for whom "How are you" is not merely a social nicety, compatriots who speak the same language that others find foreign. Manfred has taken to writing poetry about what he has lost, and he shares his poems with me. He once gave me a photocopy of a saying he found: There is no joy the world can give like that it takes away. I have painted these words on a wall in our house, beneath a kind of collage framed in birch branches. At the center of the work is a ceramic tile on which is painted a Chagall-like image of a woman, with a simple, tranquil face, holding a man in her arms. They lie together, as if floating on water, surrounded by flowers and leaves which trail from a branch held in the man's hand. His face is not visible, buried in her hair. I had pressed the flowers of my wedding bouquet, and for four years they remained between the pages of a heavy book. These I glued around the tile, and in one corner is a little red cement heart, a gift Don had given to his friends one year for Valentine's Day. I then covered the surface with a piece of translucent rice paper, to soften the image. It makes some people uncomfortable, this saying written right on the wall, too pessimistic for them perhaps, but I know it to be true. There are losses that are irreplaceable.

I tire of hearing, "You'll meet someone new." Maybe I will, maybe I won't, but that is not the point. It will not diminish what I have lost. Life cannot replace what death has stolen. Paul's missing years, and mine, are gone forever. If there comes someday a happy ending, it will arrive on an undercurrent of sorrow, and it will be stained by fear. I still, at times, envy Paul the role he played in this drama.

My life is a dichotomy; the schism between private and public is wide and deep. Not this year, but maybe the next, a friend at work tells me how well I'm doing, that I'm funny and seem like my old self. It amazes me that the façade is so opaque, that the lost days aren't visible in my eyes, that I have become a proficient actress, the one theatrical skill I never had the urge to master. It saddens me to realize that no one knows me well enough to see that it's all pretense. And yet . . . As a child, I was painfully shy. As an adult, I sought to overcome this personality trait by using what I thought of as the "Whistle a Happy Tune" method. It sounds unbearably trite, but it worked. The song is from the musical *The King and I*, and it is Anna's solution for overcoming fear. Anna, coincidentally, was a young widow, living in a foreign land. The pertinent line is: "The result of this deception is very strange to tell, for when I fool the people I fear, I fool myself as well." So I pretended not to be shy for long enough that people thought of me as self-confident, until I believed it myself, and the fiction became reality. Sometimes, very rarely, I feel like that small child attempting to be brave, but mostly it is who I have become.

Acting cheerful has turned into the same process. At first, it was a defense. To let people see my pain was an invasion of privacy, an opening when all I wanted was to close myself off. I hid behind wit and humor, until I realized with a shock and a pang that it was no longer a lie, that smiles were no longer the public version of tears but had a sweetness of their own, that the brief glints of happiness no longer felt like betrayal.

As I reentered the land of the living, I was aware that I was creating a new person from the ashes, someone very similar to the old me, but forged from steel. At times I feel so strong, so invincible, that I am amazed when the sorrows of daily life hurt me, just as they would anyone else. It comes as a surprise that my heart can still be broken. And now that I see the lives of others more clearly, instead of through the distortion of my own grief, I realize that even a life that has not been destroyed by tragedy can be deeply poignant, that even the small blows encountered in a normal life can cause pain, that other losses hurt. Where once I was impatient with those unhappy with what seemed like so much, now I pity them for choosing sorrow when they could have joy, but I also know that options are often limited and choices are sometimes complicated.

I find that I have become more honest and therefore more

difficult. I say what I think, losing friends along the way, but unwilling to go back for them, not feeling that I should apologize. Like Paul not wasting kisses, I will not waste time on empty social rituals, and so I end up spending my time alone. I envy acquaintances for whom friendship comes easily, but I treasure the few close friends I have. Sometimes it seems that each one fulfills a need, and although, when they are all put together, they may fall short of the best friend who has gone missing, their love and support have helped fill the void, and for that I feel blessed.

APRIL 1991

Spring can't help but get under my skin. When I moved in with Paul, I thought I liked the neighborhood well enough as half of a couple, but for a single woman I feared it might be too far off the beaten track. My parents hinted that a move might do me good, give me a fresh outlook. They didn't know how excruciating apartment hunting in New York City was. Even if it weren't, I wasn't ready to leave, to relinquish those sudden, breathtaking images of Paul standing in the kitchen, or walking into the bedroom.

I almost never go out in the evenings, so it doesn't matter that there are no movie theatres, no restaurants, no interesting stores. What there is is a beautiful park set atop the stately cliffs that line the Hudson River. Terraced gardens frame promenades that weave their way to the Cloisters, a museum created from the remnants of European monasteries. John D. Rockefeller, Jr., bought, or plundered, depending on one's point of view, these ruins and donated them to the city of New York. He also purchased the cliff on the far side of the river and made it public land, with the stipulation that nothing be built higher than the tree line, so that now, all these years later, in this densely populated area, lies a sweep of what appears to be wilderness.

I remember swimming this stretch of river; it was one of my favorites. Spuyten Duyvil, a narrow canal from the Harlem River, opens into the expansive Hudson. The park land on either side gives the impression, especially from the water, that one has slipped backwards into the nineteenth century, or earlier. If I didn't lift my head to see the George Washington Bridge three miles downstream, I could pretend there were Indians watching from behind trees, or settlers on horseback riding the ridges. I like living in an area that I first saw from the water. It is a quiet neighborhood, many of the residents elderly refugees from Germany, the younger families from Russia. I love the stories the older people share with me, envious of these tiny people who have grown old together, empathetic with the many feisty women alone.

Paul and I tried to walk through the park at least every other day in the spring. Masses of flowers blossomed in waves of color. As the crocuses died, they were replaced by daffodils and azaleas, then tulips and scilla, then peonies and poppies. At first it was difficult to walk in the park by myself. Eventually, after countless trips to the Cloisters and back, I feel that I am wearing grooves in the pavement. With my Walkman to drive the thoughts from my head and dark sunglasses to hide my tortured eyes, I wander through autumn and winter into spring, the season that finally gets to me, the time of year when I fall in love again, two years in a row, even though neither adventure lasted the summer.

Three and half years after Paul's death, I had a simple affair. It wasn't the sort of thing that was meant to last; we were both aware of the limitations of personality, and lives heading in opposite directions. Even so, the end wasn't simple. But we remain friends, and I will always be fond of him. There was pain at the time, but it was mostly that of returning from a pleasant detour to my lonely path. The second man, whom I met in the spring of the following year, was the one who swept me away before fleeing, the one who reminded me I still had a heart capable of being broken.

Life and men have changed in the ten years since I last dated, and so have I. Or maybe I have forgotten, although, when I think back, I remember how I hated going out with strangers, disliked parties. Because I traveled in circles where few wed young, I hadn't learned to be wary of married men who don't wear wedding bands. I tire of discussions on the dearth of decent available men, but it is a problem, as is my inclination toward solitude. "You have a lot going for you," friends assure me. "Self-confidence isn't the issue," I reply. The odds against finding true love twice seem insurmountable, but I refuse to deny the possibility, the hope. I know exactly which years of my life were best.

It seems that I am almost alone among my friends in believing in the possibility of deep, lasting love, never having experienced the wearing away of a long marriage. How can it be so bad, I wonder, when they can talk to their spouses, reach out and touch them, fall asleep beside them. In some ways I feel so simple and childish when I listen to the sad tales of their complicated lives. "You don't understand," says one woman. "You weren't married very long." Well, no. No, I wasn't.

Our anniversary. It would have been our third. There are too many double-trouble dates. The year we were married, May 8 fell on Mother's Day, so we felt as though we had two anniversaries, which seemed nice the two years we celebrated together. Then there were Paul's two birthdays, although I think I have a firmer grasp on the correct date than he ever did, or his parents. And I think of Paul's death as occurring on August 8, though officially, on the death certificate, it was recorded as August 9. Instead of spreading the bad days out, all this confusion just creates more of them.

Anniversaries and birthdays serve as milestones. Because they are more easily remembered, the incremental, faltering steps that count as progress become evident. The rest of the year is a boundless sea; I think I am moving forward, but it could be a mirage. Days that are significant pass like markers on the shore. This year I sleepwalk through this day; the next year I am able to work, albeit quietly, keeping to myself. Seven years after our marriage, I can actually bear to remember our wedding day, how nervous I was during the ceremony, how I left too much wine in the glass, so that Paul turned bright red when he gulped it down, and everyone laughed, how my sister fumbled for Paul's ring because our bouquets were so bountiful that she didn't have a free hand, and they laughed some more, how Paul teased my darling Aunt Sara for her hand gestures, always pointing to emphasize her words, how it felt to dance the first dance in his arms, the way we had practiced in our living room, and how it was our first night together as husband and wife. The memories come closer the farther away I go, as if they were always there, waiting for me to be ready to recall them, to bring them back from banishment.

There are too many people missing from our wedding-album pictures. Most of them would still be young today, or ten years from today, or twenty.

JUNE 1991

Over the winter, I planned the future of Paul's cemetery. The previous fall, Gregg had woven branches into a fence around the grave and the oak sapling which, though it had grown no taller, had not let go of its few dry leaves. The form was that of an infinity symbol, with one loop encircling the tree, and the other the cobblestone marker. It was lovely but temporary. I paced out an area roughly twenty-five square feet and placed a rock at each corner, visualizing the stone wall that would connect the points, and the swath of flowers that would border the center lawn. One spring day, with a fine mist softening the air, my neighbors brought over their Rototiller and, father and son, took turns digging up the earth around the perimeter.

My soil was not rocky, and after several forays into the woods with a wheelbarrow, I realized that if this was not to become a life project, I would have to find another source for my stone wall. Bob and Marie, who were in their sixties and were fondly known as "the hermits," lived far back in the hills in a house they had built from trees they had cut down without power tools and hand-hewn into beams. It was they who had found the oak sapling to plant, and they who had dug the holes for both the tree and Paul's grave. I was ready to find a stone quarry, to buy what I needed to create a wall and have it delivered, but they suggested that I find a rock slide near the road, so I could use my car for hauling. They didn't understand why I would want to pay for something that could be obtained for free, with a little exertion.

I explored the back roads near my house and found the perfect spot about nine miles away where the cliff had been blasted out to make the road decades before. The rocks were a beautiful mixture of foggy gray and sea-green shot through with the sparkle of mica, reminiscent of light on water, and the deep blood red, almost black, of garnet. I opened the hatchback of my tiny car and lifted as many boulders as I thought safe into it. The best ones were of course the biggest, and the biggest ones were of course the heaviest. On the chance that taking rocks wasn't strictly legal, and because there was no place at the side of the road to pull off, I worked in the early morning.

The spring had been quite warm and the water in Paradox Lake was very bearable as early as the beginning of June. I caught myself thinking how lucky I had been that the previous year had been so much colder, the better to train to swim the English Channel. I was torn between Paradox and New York City, driving back and forth between the two, not sure where I wanted to be, fearing that I was reverting to not wanting to be anywhere, finally forcing myself to choose.

The Summer of the Monarch Butterflies. I decided I deserved a couple of months in the Adirondacks. A few teachers I knew summered in the mountains. It seemed so civilized to me, so appealing. The royalty check from the *Backstage Handbook* would see me through for a few months. When people hear that I spend my summers in the Adirondacks, and invariably say, "You're so lucky!" I can't help but think, and sometimes retort, "Luck has nothing to do with it." New York City in the summer feels too much like death to me.

Packing my bags blindsided me. It had seemed understandable that I be upset the day I left for England without Paul; I didn't expect to be brought to my knees every time I place clothes into a suitcase, or check a list of things to bring. In five years, with five summers spent in Paradox, this has not changed, no matter how I try. At least now I know, which helps. As the day I have chosen for leaving approaches, I become restless, agitated. I run around the city trying to take care of ridiculous chores. I think about staying longer, waiting until the next week to leave, until suddenly I can take no more wavering and, in a mad rush, pack up, grab the turtle, and hit the road.

Bob and Marie had noticed the rocks I had gathered and

started placing in the field. Bob is color-blind, but Marie thought they were pretty and asked me where I found them. When I told her, she asked if I would mind if she helped me. Mind?! She needed something to do in the early mornings before Bob awoke. She had already chopped enough wood for the next ten years, and without a project, time weighed heavy on her hands. I had mentioned that I usually went between 6:30 and 7:00. She thought 6:00 sounded perfect. No matter how many times we drove that road, each time it looked different. It wound its way through the woods; the early-morning light drizzled through the trees as it melted the fog. Deer grazed placidly in sunny fields, rabbits leapt through dewy grass. Cardinal flowers blazed red beside cool, dark streams; flashes of blue cobalt were scattered across the road, remnants from a time when iron mines lined the valley.

Marie taught me the smart way to move heavy objects. We kept a two-by-twelve in the car to use as a ramp and together rolled the largest rocks up it, into the hatchback. At first I tried to protect the inside of the car. After a while, in satisfied anger, I watched as the rocks scraped and gouged scars into the plastic. Paul and I bought that car together when our old one was stolen two months after we were married. He was always annoyed whenever I dripped paint in the car; this was another petty way to get back at him for leaving. It was important to him to keep the car nice; I trashed it. I treated it like a pickup truck; he thought of it as a luxury sedan. But I do love that car, more so as it shows its age.

Today it has many miles on it and serious rust problems. The right rear taillight leaks, and has since we bought it, so after the rain I try to remember to bail out the wheel well, but usually forget until the sound of sloshing rusty water reminds me. The back is a different color from the front, the result of a bad paint job after a rear-end collision that occurred while Paul was stopped at a red light in Connecticut. As Marie and I drove back along the rough road, we tried to ignore the creaking and groaning. I maneuvered across the ruts in the field, as close to the garden as possible. Once I landed on top of a rock buried in the grass and had to jack the car up to pull it out. The exhaust system needed to be replaced the following autumn. By then I was determined to repair the car at any cost, to keep it forever.

By eight or nine in the morning it was usually too hot to continue, and Marie would be anxious to get back in time to make Bob's breakfast. The rocks accumulated. Every few days, Bob would come over in the afternoon with Marie and we'd build the wall. They told me it would have to be at least two layers thick or it would fall down. As we worked, Bob and Marie argued. "You can't put that rock like that. You're burying the colorful side. Can't you see that?" she harangued.

"Sorry," Bob said, chuckling sheepishly. "They just look like rocks to me."

Their voices eddied around me as I got stuck where I was, trying to make the wall too perfect, unable to work out how this boulder would fit here until I put it there, only to find that it didn't match at all. They never seemed to notice that their side grew, strong and beautiful, while mine waxed and waned, but progressed incrementally. On days they didn't come, I took apart what I had done, determined to make it better, willing to try as many times as it took to get it right, unable to settle. The sun beat down, baking the field, scorching the hay. It was too hot, I thought, for shoes, so I wore flip-flops, even as I told myself how stupid I was. Each time I inevitably smashed a toe, it was almost a relief; I knew I had it coming, now I no longer had to wait for the pain. While there alone, I spent almost as much time lying on my back in the grass, daydreaming, resting. Looking up at all that sky, watching the breeze sweep across the field, I floated, felt myself grow calm, resigned, accepting of what was.

There is a black-and-white photograph that someone took of Lottie, Heather, and myself sitting on a finished part of the wall, with rocks strewn haphazardly around us. I joke that it just goes to show that widows come in all shapes and sizes. I talk to these two friends about things that no one else can truly understand. Others try to empathize by telling of divorces or broken love affairs or the death of a parent, and I want to say, "But after the divorce, you could call your husband on the phone and hear his voice, so how does that relate to me?" or "Did you fall asleep every night in the arms of your mother or father, whispering things no one else knew?" One woman, whenever she stopped by to visit, talked of all that had gone wrong in her life, or distant friends who had died, or were ill. When I asked her why, she replied that she wanted me to know that other people had hardships in their lives. How was I supposed to benefit from knowing these things? I knew that no life is without problems but gleaned no comfort from this fact.

Heather tells how it was to carry a cup of tea to her ailing husband as he lay in bed, with a cold, they thought, only to see him go into the convulsions of cardiac arrest. And Lottie tells of accompanying her cancer-stricken husband to the hospital one day, then returning home to care for her children, thinking she would be able to speak to him the next morning. But when she arrived back at the hospital there was only time to exchange a glance as he was rolled into the operating room, where he was put on life support, never to speak again, or open his eyes. These were the hardships that had meaning for me; these were the friends who made sense to me. We could joke about things no one else would find funny, deride people like the co-worker who two months after Rick's death told Heather she needed to get on with her life, or the super in our building who said the same to me, adding that Paul would have wanted it—as if he knew Paul, or me, as if by waking up every morning I wasn't doing exactly that. We laughed at clichés, even though we wanted to hurt the people who offered them as wisdom, or advice. We scoffed at the man who told us we shouldn't think of ourselves as "widows"—that was in the past. A lot of things are in the past, that doesn't mean they're over and done with. We were as cruel to others among ourselves as they were unknowingly to us. It was a relief to say these things aloud.

The stone wall has created its own ecosystem. In the center of the field creatures now live, having found shelter within the confines of the rocks—an iridescent green frog with dark spots, a garter snake that basks in the sun, slithering into the coolness of the wall when I inadvertently disturb it, robins and sparrows and bluebirds that splash about in the birdbath when I remember to fill it with water. The hummingbirds, butterflies, and bees come for the flowers, many of which were chosen for their names—forget-me-nots, bleeding hearts, love-in-a-mist, love-lies-bleeding. There is even a dwarf willow called Weeping Sally in the plant catalogue. The first one I ordered died within a few weeks. The company replaced it, as they do anything that doesn't last a season, and the new one has done well these past few years, although the trunk is strangely curved. It should probably be staked, to ensure that it grow straight and tall—to its projected height of six feet—but I am curious to see what will happen to it if it's left alone.

There are meadow rue and baptisia, because these were our favorite flowers in the park near our apartment. There are roses, including "sea foam" and "Paul's Himalayan musk," and others which I love for their beauty and their scent, and respect for their thorns. There are plantings that friends have given me from their own gardens. When I am offered seedlings, I always explain my palette—no orange, no yellow, except small touches and stamens. My scenic artist friends understand this, but my friend Judy was startled, and amused.

A year and a half after Paul died, before Judy knew about my color aversions, her husband plowed and seeded my field to grow grain for their sheep. She laughingly said it was lucky he had planted alfalfa, which has purple flowers. This conversation took place in the fall. The following spring, when seedlings had started growing, I arrived for my first visit after dark. Climbing stiffly out of the car, I was intoxicated, as always, by the scent of pine and the freshness of the air. It was a soft, balmy evening.

Before spending much time in the country, when I read Thomas Hardy novels set in the rural England of the nineteenth century, I wondered how those people went visiting at ten o'clock at night, how they managed to see as they traipsed along unlit paths after dark. Now I know that even on a moonless night the starlight can be quite bright. The Milky Way, in the summer, arcs across my field, running straight down the valley. Objects may not have color in the moonlight, but they do cast shadows, and sometimes, under the full moon, I would swear that the barns are still red.

I walked through the field, breathing deeply; I was halfway to the garden before my eyes adjusted to the dimness. Enthralled, I looked into the night at a blanket of pale flowers glowing through the dark, whispering in the breeze. I opened the garden gate, paid my respects, then wandered back and forth across the field, unable, for a long time, to go inside.

The next morning I awoke and walked out to the balcony off the sleeping loft. The field was a sea of foamy yellow, the flowers composed of ethereal petals that floated above wispy foliage. When Judy saw me, later that day, she apologized profusely for landing me with acres of yellow flowers. I laughed, and assured her I loved them, that they were actually a beautiful color. Sometimes, near Lake Placid, there is a field of sunflowers that is spectacular. Just because I wouldn't want them in my garden doesn't mean I don't appreciate their beauty. The wild mustard, for that is what had somehow grown, was the perfect surround for the blues and purples and whites of my garden. It never reappeared after that summer, except for a few persistent renegades, mostly within the wall, and those I weed out.

There are plants that don't survive, that won't return after an Adirondack winter, bulbs that never bloomed. I had sowed an all-white spring garden. All I ever saw of it was a handful of tulip buds that the deer usually ate before they opened. Some things I keep around, even though they never flower, never thrive, just because they show up faithfully every spring. There were a few plants that I plowed under, or dug up, as I shall perhaps do with that sorry oak tree, no bigger now than it was five years ago, and obviously struggling. It is a sickly reminder; I would rather see a healthy tree, preferably something that flowers, and weeps, and can withstand the cold. Each year I think, I'll plant something new in the spring, but then when I arrive the tiny tree is covered with leaves and I haven't the heart to uproot it. Marie warns me that if the tree actually grows to its full potential, I won't want it there, for it will shade my garden.

I still struggle over an epitaph for an as yet undesigned grave marker. As time passes and my perspective changes, the various choices I make no longer seem right by the time I think about actually acting on them. I can find no lines of poetry that are absolutely right, and can write none of my own that would suffice. I know Paul would not be pleased with what is there now —a cobblestone scavenged from a New York City street with his name printed on it neatly, along with the date of his birth, and his death, and simply the word "Beloved." It bothers me, and amuses me, that it is done in Magic Marker, and must be relettered each year, as it fades away, even though the ink is supposed to be permanent. The spot is waiting, ringed with rocks left over from the wall, lined with white marble tiles. Friends in the valley have placed stones on the grave, a Jewish tradition that I never knew about. The old cemeteries that I haunt, looking for inspiration, are so much more beautiful than new ones, the gravestones softened by time and moss, the carving so obviously done by hand, the imperfection adding character. I will not settle for a laser-cut slab of granite.

Sometime after Paul died, my friends from the Macy's parade studio wrote me a card, telling me they had something for me. I was perplexed. The thought of a gift on the occasion of my husband's death seemed odd. Months went by and I was told it was a birdbath, for Paradox. So I stopped in Hoboken on my way upstate one day and they loaded it into the car for me. It is cement, on a traditional pedestal. The ivy I planted at its base never grew, and I wish it would look older faster, but so far I've refrained from using any scenic artistry to help it along. At first, I never saw the birds actually using it, but I knew they had been there from the feathers floating on the water, and when I approached the garden, the air was crowded with fleeing birds. Now I often catch them splashing around, each one waiting its turn, perched on the edge.

My feet have forged a narrow, winding path from which I do not stray the many times each day I visit my garden. It slices through the tall grass, a wrinkled crease in the smoothly undulating field. Each summer, as I first walk the route, I think I am scribing a straight line, only to be bemused by the gentle curves and twists clearly visible from the back porch.

I knew I would want some kind of seat there, because this place had become another room in my house. After Don died, I bought a bench he had made, from his lover, Edgardo. It had been in the garden of the country home they shared until Don became too weak to go there, and Edgardo was forced to rent it, then sell it, before he, too, died. Don worked as a graphic designer, but mostly what he did was create things out of unusual materials—address books made of metal, photo albums sandwiched between two slices of wood, tabletops poured from cement. Our wedding present was a series of interlocking concrete slabs, blue and green and gray, that formed a table. I asked him to make two small tables for me for Paradox. Both have cement tops on iron bases. One is pale blue, like the sky on certain days, with iridescent ceramic stars scattered, embedded, across it. The other one is sand-colored, with bits of shells and stones visible in the smooth surface.

The garden bench Don made that I now have started as a traditional wooden bench, with a back of vertical slats, and arms. Don bought it without the seat, and made his own by pouring cement over richly colored, glistening glass shards. It is completely flat, but sometimes people are reluctant to sit on it, not believing that they won't be cut to shreds. I love to end my days on this bench, with a book and a glass of wine. The sun disappears into the trees long before it sets, so I rarely see spectacular sunsets, but the warm memory of the hidden light is enough. It has to be. I can't imagine ever letting go of this place.

In this garden, I have regained some of the easiness I felt with Paul, some of the teasing, as when I cut the grass around his grave with the noisy, reeking-of-gasoline lawn mower that he spent many an afternoon with. "Bet you like this a lot, huh?" I say to myself, to Paul. Every so often, when I'm watering the flowers, by accident I turn the hose on his grave, at which point I laughingly wince and apologize. I send him a casual "Hey, honey" when I open the gate, and a fond farewell on my way out. I visit him as soon as I arrive in Paradox, and promise I'll be back soon as I leave. I lie in the grass beside him, and look up at the sky, or close my eyes. It's not that I think he's there, more than anywhere else. It's that this place is his, and mine, and was created as a result of his death, different from the space we shared in life, specific to all that his absence has meant.

The summer we built the wall, I didn't swim much until it was finished. My shoulders and legs and back ached from lifting rocks. I would slip into the lake to cool off, often returning home to sleep through the afternoon heat. When I swam, I did it at day's end, and stayed between the dock and the island. Every so often, when Marie decided we had enough rocks gathered to take a day off, I did my regular swim, to the narrows and back, about two miles. It seemed so long to me, where once it had been little more than a warm-up.

One weekend, when friends were helping build the wall, Lottie pointed out a monarch-butterfly chrysalis. It was a pale jade drop with gold markings, very elegant-looking. The field was overgrown with milkweed that year before the phantom alfalfa was planted. Next she found a monarch-butterfly caterpillar— white, black, and yellow-striped. As we started searching, we saw more and more caterpillars eating their way around the milkweed leaves. Eventually, the chrysalises were everywhere, hanging from the undersides of rocks left in the field overnight, in every nook and cranny of the wall, under the deck, on the window muntins. I saw the caterpillars attach themselves, then go into their hook-shaped trance, watched as they pumped themselves into their glistening cocoons.

After a few weeks, the outside darkened and became transparent, revealing the brilliant orange-and-yellow patterns inside. I became expert at predicting when the butterflies would emerge, after spending hours waiting for those first cracks in the shells. The creatures were almost frightening when they crawled forth, misshapen, with enormous bodies and tiny, intensely bright wings. They climbed to a quiet place and rearranged themselves into something beautiful, and graceful, before flying away.

By the time the monarch butterflies started emerging, I had finished the wall and moved on to painting the trim on the house. None of the colors at the paint store was right, so I talked the owner into mixing a special color, which he named "spruce teal." It still wasn't exactly perfect, so I tinted it at home. I wanted a deep, rich blue-green with a sense of age, a feeling that it had once been more vibrant. I started a monarch-butterfly hospital for the chrysalises that had chosen the trim for their incubation. I carefully sliced the "stems" off the wood and push-pinned them to a better spot. Not all of the transplants survived, but many did. Indeed, many of the chrysalises in the field never opened. They went through all the normal stages, darkened into transparency, and then nothing more happened. Or sometimes the butterflies emerged, but with a bent wing that never straightened, making flight impossible. I tried to nurse them as best I could, moving them to sheltered spots out of harm's way, but they persisted in wandering off. Others seemed almost friendly. As I was on a ladder, painting, one sunny afternoon, an especially brilliantly colored butterfly attached itself to the underside of my arm and stayed there as I painted, gently, so as not to disturb it.

How could I not see these magical occurrences as signs, of healing, if nothing else? One evening, or maybe morning, but the light was low and fresh, I walked through the field and raised a cloud of butterflies that had been hidden in the milkweed.

Surrounded, I was enchanted. The butterflies never returned in those numbers after that summer.

I am realizing the subtle ways in which Paul changed me, without trying, fascinated by this person I somehow became without noticing. One afternoon, some years before, one of our neighbors had stopped by and asked what our plans were for the afternoon. We had, in fact, just been discussing that. I said, peevishly, "I think we should go out and do something fun, but Paul doesn't know how to relax. He wants to work on the house."

Paul replied, "Maybe that's because your idea of relaxation is climbing a mountain, then going canoeing, then swimming five miles." Our discussion was the source of much amusement for our neighbor, and for us. Somewhere along the way I adopted Paul's satisfaction in puttering. Our house, which was once just someplace to stay between swims and hikes, is now an end in itself, a constant, ongoing, never-ending project, a distraction. I finally built the bed we hadn't gotten around to, having spent years sleeping on a futon on the floor. I consulted Paul as I figured out how to make it, apologized for my not-quite-square cuts, telling him if he thought he could do it better he should do it himself, taking pride in balancing the sheets of plywood on sawhorses so I could lean over the balcony and pull them up myself, scavenging birch logs for legs. I feel lucky to have these skills, sorry for widows who suddenly find themselves helpless in practical terms. Many years ago, my friend Jenna asked what I would do when the house was finished. I looked at her as if she was out of her mind, knowing that it never would be.

One afternoon I arrive, hot and tired, for a cool-off dip at Lottie's. There are people on the deck, so I try to be sociable, say hello. One young woman asks me, "Don't you get lonely back there, all by yourself?" My eyes open wide, so startled that all I can do is shrug and try to control the tears. Social niceties are once again beyond me; I try to reassure her that it doesn't matter, then start walking slowly down the long path to the water. There are footsteps behind me. Annoyed, I turn around to see a young boy whose family is renting Lottie's extra cabin for the week. My smile is more of a grimace. I do not want company.

He follows me onto the dock. He asks me if I am going to swim, as I take off my T-shirt and shorts, tells me he is learning how back home. I am on the verge of escaping into the water. "Do you take swimming lessons?" he asks me. Laughter and tears fill my eyes simultaneously; what a question to ask me! I dive into the water, suddenly enjoying myself. I swim a little, showing off, then do flip turns near the end of the dock, to splash the boy, whose name is Chris. Later, he proudly introduces me to his parents, his new friend, Sally, who knows how to swim. We establish a tradition between us, this summer and those that follow. When he hears my car in the morning as I arrive, he wakes up. Sometime after I have swum away, he ambles down to the lake with his fishing pole, to wait for me. He stands at the very end of the dock as I approach. I pretend not to see him. As close as is safe, I do as splashy a flip turn as I can, spraying him with as much water as possible. I look up and say, "Oh, I'm sorry! I didn't know you were standing there!" Just to make him laugh.

I have known deep satisfaction in time spent with the children of others. I often babysat for the stepdaughter of the woman who sold me my house. Instead of reimbursing me, she deducted money from my mortgage payments. I grew to love this girl, then known as Jenny, now as Jenna. Paul and I would take her tobogganing with us; then he sat happily reading as she and I played Scrabble, more and more intensely as the years went by. One day, after Paul died, while she was in college, we sat visiting beside the wood stove, and she asked me, "How do you know when love is real?" I answered as best I could, and tried to keep the tears of affection from my eyes, sensing the joys that could be had in watching a beloved child age. She is now a very dear friend, more so because I knew the girl she was.

For the past few years, my neighbor Elizabeth, who just turned thirteen, has visited often, riding over on her bicycle, calling me to see if I'll give her a swimming lesson, and I feel the process repeating itself. One day, a very bad day, she stopped by. I had been crying, my eyes were bloodshot and puffy, my cheeks were wet. I barely opened the door, only halfway, and asked her to come back another time. She wouldn't let me close the door. Putting a foot inside, in case I tried, she said, "You look like you need a hug," and proceeded to give me one, wisely ignoring the tears running down my face. I wiped my eyes and let her in. It just so happened that she had brought me a present, a pair of turtle earrings. She asked me which ones I wanted, those with the blue stones or those with the black. I suggested that we each take one of each, so we could really share them. By the time she left, my heart was immeasurably lighter. She once showed me a homework assignment on goals for the coming years. Swimming across Schroon Lake was on her list.

Sometimes, when I call Los Angeles and my sister answers, I

ask her to put Molly on the phone. She doesn't have to ask why; she knows. My niece never met her Uncle Paul, although she was at his funeral. When I hear her cheerful little "Hel-lo-ow," and her stories about her baby brother, or her imaginary older brothers, or what she did at kindergarten, sometimes it is enough.

A U G U S T   5 ,   1 9 9 1

This time last year Paul was alive. I am more and more agitated as the anniversary of his death approaches. I recently had a dream. Paul was swimming in Paradox Lake, in the cove beyond Lottie's dock. Suddenly there appeared a huge truck, a semi, driving in circles on the water around him, churning up whitecaps, leaving a terrible wake, swinging nearer and nearer to Paul as the vortex closed in. I tried to scream, to warn him, but it was one of those soundless cries that can't be forced out through sleep, until finally I awoke, gasping, incoherent.

On this morning, the lake is flat and dark, the sky pewter with low-hanging clouds, the air still. I swim down the center, as I always do, secure in knowing that I, and my wake, and my safety orange cap, are eminently visible. I see a boat slowly approaching. It is an aluminum rowboat with a motor. The weight of the three men, from their beer bellies, their arrogance, and their self-righteousness, causes the vessel to ride low in the water, to appear as if it were sinking. I know that they are just coming over for a closer look and am annoyed. I don't like boats to come too close. I stop swimming, to make sure they see me, although I know they have.

When they are near enough to be heard clearly, they start yelling, "What do you think you're doing out here by yourself? Do you have any idea how hard it is to see you? New York State law says you have to be accompanied by a boat. Are you crazy? Stupid?" In truth, I don't remember every word, but that was the gist of it. I have no idea why I infuriated them so, and don't really care. I cannot bear to be yelled at. I could think of no response, although I've thought of plenty since, and it didn't matter anyway, since as soon as they were done with their bullying they lumbered off. I was pretty shaken up, at least partially because they were three and I was one, and there was only one reason I could think of at the time why I was out there in the middle of the lake, or anywhere, alone. I turned back, swam to the dock, pulled myself out, wrapped myself in my towel, and sobbed, the convulsive, gulping kind, the sort that left me helpless for the rest of the day.

It didn't take long for my reaction to turn to anger and rebellion. I wasn't going to let three idiots ruin what I loved best. The next week I went into Schroon Lake and bought the biggest, brightest beach ball I could find. I tied it to a string and rigged it to a Velcro strap which I now wear around my ankle whenever I swim. I won't give anyone a chance to berate me, or say I'm difficult to see, ever again, and I don't particularly care if it looks silly. When boats come close I refuse to stop. I keep my head down and swim on. I know the rules about swimming alone and they don't apply to me. I have swum thousands of miles and never had a debilitating cramp. I don't see why I should have to swim close to the shore—that's where the creepy-crawlies are. And besides, I need to be surrounded by open water. Like a cowboy riding the range, I think, Don't fence me in.

Forty-eight of the really long kind of hours. I don't see how time can be an absolute, how sixty seconds can always equal a minute, how each of those seconds can be of the same duration, how they can each have the same weight in the context of that minute. There was one second when Paul was alive, walking through the summer heat, then there was the next one, which lasted an eternity for him, long enough that he put out his hands to break his fall, to stop time, but broke his wrists instead. And the ramifications of that split-second decision, which was made so quickly that it barely qualifies as a choice, to run the light instead of braking, will never be completely known. I haven't a clue about how it has affected the driver. I don't waste my thoughts on him. My only revenge is in knowing his nightmares must be worse than mine. And if not, it doesn't matter. It is not accurate to think of it as an accident, for it had a cause, carelessness, and an effect, Paul's death. It was unintentional, no doubt, but from my point of view, that is not a mitigating factor. Absolution is not a familiar concept to me. Instead, I put the crucial instant from my mind, although sometimes it sneaks into my imagination until, horrified, I banish it, and reserve my energy for the time that follows.

Every year, I think that this year, these days will be easier.

And every year, they are not. The first year was only bearable thanks to a Valium and the sleep that resulted. Another year I was half out of my mind with loneliness, struggling to finish a revised edition of Paul's book, wondering what on earth possessed me to consent to this torture. I called Betsy, who hopped into her car and drove up for one of the bad days. We hiked up the "Brothers," over to Big Slide, and back down. It was a wonderfully tiring way to make the time pass. I know I should do this more often when I see trouble coming—arrange diversions —but here it is, August 8 again, a beautiful, crystal-clear, absolutely miserable day in the Adirondacks. And too late to do anything about it; Betsy is away on vacation; other friends are either at work or with their spouses or families. Most of them don't even realize what day this is. After only five years, my sister and my parents have forgotten the significance of this date, although my sister apologizes profusely when I remind her, and, two months later, makes sure that I know she remembers Paul's birthday. I will never forget this anniversary, always sense it lurking come August, waiting to pounce and drag me under. Someday, maybe, I will have learned that it won't pass by easily and plan accordingly.

As a way to kill the day this year, I walk to Goose Pond, at the base of Pharaoh Mountain, to swim. All these places are saturated with memories. As I sit on my favorite rock, drowsily letting the sun dry my body, I think of a time we came here, Paul and I, and two swimming friends. As so often happened, the three of us swam far away, while Paul waited, enjoying a quiet read. When we arrived and scrambled out of the water, he was excited, agitated almost. A branch, a very large branch, had fallen off a tree and landed right beside him. I climbed higher, to where he was, and saw it, and knew fear, even though the danger was past. "Did you have any warning? How did you move in time?"

"There was a crack, but I didn't know it was right there. And it's just as well I didn't move, because it didn't hit me." We joked that swimming off to the middle of nowhere was a lot safer than sitting on a rock reading a book. I could tell Paul was a little shaken, though he wouldn't admit it, but his relief was obvious, and his delight in his luck.

AUGUST 12, 1991

Water temperature is much less forgiving than air temperature. There is a very small range of what is comfortable for swimming, only about 10 degrees for most people. In air, the difference between what is pleasant and what is not is far greater. This has to do with the physical properties of air and water, the fact that water is denser and affects the body more. A body cools much more rapidly in water, although water itself cools much less rapidly than air. It would take a long time to freeze to death in 60-degree air, but not long at all, relatively speaking, in 60-degree water.

One long, hot summer, the water off Lottie's dock reached 82 degrees. I could barely move my arms, my stroke count felt as if it were half of what was normal for me. I was unable to swim every day, and sometimes only as far as Birch Island. I longed for cold water, instead of that lethargy-inducing quagmire. I knew that if I were to try to swim fast, it would only make me nauseous, like running in 100-degree air. It was the kind of water that was perfect for lying on a raft, for floating through the midday heat, for teaching a child to swim. The warmth seemed to make the liquid unbelievably soft, like a balmy breeze on an early-spring day, soothing with the kindness of unexpected gentleness. "Take it easy," I told myself. "Relax." But I couldn't wait for the water to cool, even though I might regret my complaints when it did.

As the night air chills, the morning fog lasts later and later, until it seems it will never leave. I wait for it to lift, first at my house as I sip my coffee, then on the dock. Often my valley is bursting with light while Paradox Lake is still draped in gauze. I bring something to read, and wait, shivering lightly in the damp. Once the sun starts to burn through, there is not much time left. Each trip is an attempt to achieve perfect timing. Swimming through the fog is lovely but the obscurity cannot be so complete that finding my way is difficult. I await the change in density that signals the end is near. As long as I can see each reference point in its turn—Crawford Island, the edge of the bay, Grass Island—it is clear enough. If I have done it right, there are still the barest memories of haze left for my return. A sense of loss descends with the dissipation of the fog. The sun seems so harsh, the bright daylight boring. I prefer the oblique light of early morning or evening, or that which is filtered through mist, or hovers before or after rain, the kind of light that presages change, or follows it.

By the end of August, Lottie's house is deserted. I park my car at the top of the hill, walk down the wooden stairway, then the steep path to the log steps. Lottie keeps her land much as it was a hundred years ago. Whereas others along the lake have allowed the forest to take over again, her hillside is more of a meadow. The softwoods that preside over the grassy slope are stately, ancient pines. About two-thirds of the way down to the lake, there is a large log, about fifteen feet long and three feet in diameter, parallel to the path. Growing out of a cleft in the center of it is a beautiful little birch tree, leaves fluttering among all the needles. Lottie's husband had wanted his ashes scattered on Paradox Lake, which she did, mostly, but, like me, she saved some and put them in a special spot, alongside the path they always walked down to the water. She gently sprinkled them onto the mossy dirt in the gash in this log, where this perfect tree now grows.

It is finally possible to swim at the end of the day. The water-skiers have returned to college, or whatever noisy place they came from. The silent fishermen last as long as I do, and longer, no doubt, cozy in their flannel shirts and jackets. The power-boats are scarce, and seem to be there more for the beauty than for the thrill of speed, retirees enjoying the waning season. It is as tricky to judge the light as it is the fog, a challenge to swim through the best part of the sunset, to be in the water as it

235

glows crimson, drips golden from my amber arm, as the under-side of the waves darken into a metallic gleam. The temperature plummets with the sun, so it is too painful to watch, soaking wet, from the dock. I appreciate the beauty best from my van-tage point in the lake, the world lit up around me. One evening, I swam through a velvety lavender sky as the sun burned down to a dull red on one side and the full moon rose on the other, a sharp and lucid white cutting through the flamboyance. For a brief period of time, they were perfectly balanced as I turned my head to one side to breathe, then the other. That night I couldn't bear to miss one second, so I shivered in my towel until the moon won the battle for ascendancy, then lit my path as I hobbled stiffly up the hill.

SEPTEMBER

I claim the Adirondacks for myself in September. As summer matures into autumn, the tourists retreat, miss-ing the glory of sparkling days and frosty nights. The humming-birds disappear with the summer folk; the herons stay a brief while longer, until one day they, too, are gone, fleeing the en-croaching ice. I was planning to remain in Paradox only through Labor Day, but then decided to stretch it out until my birthday, and then until Paul's, which means the month of September. The weather is too perfect, the quiet too comfortable. Each year the time away lasts a little longer. It doesn't make sense to return at the beginning of October, only to drive back up for Columbus

Day. I miss the liveliness of New York City, and it makes me edgy to see nothing but white people, but I can't tear myself away from the dazzling colors of fall.

Eventually, it will be the sound of gunfire which heralds the hunting season, the sight of men walking down the road carrying rifles, or bows and arrows, the sense that it is not safe to be a woman alone in this situation, that will drive me back to New York. That, and the fact that as winter nears and the days shorten, the loneliness in Paradox feels more oppressive. My solitude is transformed from a treasure into a prison. I need to talk to people more like myself—unmarried or alone or somehow different, people who don't exist within the context of a family unit. I want to see movies and plays and hear live performances of music I love. I miss the quick wit of strangers, and friends, the random occurrences that make life interesting. As much as I love Paradox, I don't really think I'm cut out for small-town living.

In New York, I get on with my life; in Paradox, I rest. For me, it is the perfect marriage of waking and sleeping. The transitional times, the falling asleep, or awakening, will probably always be tricky, as change so often is, but once I have arrived, in Paradox for the summer, or New York for the rest of the year, I am content with the choices I have made. I so often feel like a jellyfish, swept along on currents over which I have no control, that I am surprised to realize that so much of my life is a result of conscious decisions.

In September, when I crave civilization, I drive to Saratoga, now that the crowds have departed. I enjoy the antiques stores, examining quirky objects left over from bygone times, searching for something special. One day a painting hanging high up on a wall caught my eye. The shop owner climbed a ladder to show it to me. A girl sits in a rowboat with her head bowed, her pose that of abject desolation, her hair in a long braid down her back, as mine so often is. The boat is grounded in marsh weeds, with moonlit water melting into the horizon. The colors are muddy, the painting obviously that of a not-quite-professional artist. Indeed, his name is printed on the back, followed by lists of children, and grandchildren, and great-grandchildren. It saddens me to know that I paid less than a hundred dollars for this picture, which meant that whoever sold it probably took home less than half of that. How could it not be worth more, in terms of family, if not affection, to one of his descendants? Unless, of course, somewhere in the ancestral home is a closet filled with such paintings, including some in which the colors are purer and the moonlight more sparkling. The subject matter appealed to me, but what clinched the purchase was the pencil mark that delineated the face of the girl. Elsewhere the oil paint was heavy and clumsy, but the line that separated this girl from the rest of the world was so delicate, and so touching, that I couldn't bear to let it go.

I hung the painting on my bedroom wall in Paradox, at the foot of my bed, parallel to my nun painting. My life, I thought. Two years later, a friend who sells antiques told me she often saw landscapes she thought I might like. I described the painting of the girl to her, saying that it had all the elements I look for —water, a solitary figure stooped in sorrow, a boat. Several weeks later she described a lithograph she had just seen which sounded exactly like my painting. I thought it might be a picture that an amateur would copy and asked her to buy it for me—it wasn't expensive. She brought it to work the next week. The colors were bluer, the girl smaller, the reeds more willowy, but the image was exactly the same. I took the lithograph to Paradox and hung it with pleasure above the painting. I enjoyed examining them together, to know what must have frustrated the copyist, to understand those areas of paint build-up that signal effort, if not success. But there is nothing in the professional version that has the impact of that perfect pencil line.

Several weeks later was what had become an annual event in my life, Widows' Weekend. The last weekend in September, Heather, Lottie, and I had taken to spending together in the Adirondacks. Our activities centered on an antiques sale in Blue Mountain Lake, and the fall foliage. We went hiking, sightseeing, and shopping. We usually ate dinner at a restaurant in Schroon Lake, where we ignored the other patrons as we talked and laughed and cried. This last year Lottie didn't come; her boyfriend wanted to go away somewhere else that weekend. Heather stayed at my house, which by then looked a lot like an Italian monastery, or a nunnery. I showed off my new artwork.

The next day, rummaging through a pile of junk at the antiques show, I exclaimed, "Heather! Come here! Look at this!" She was as excited as I. It was a print of the same image as those already on my wall, this time in the style of Victorian sentimentality. The waterscape was set into an oval wreathed with flowers, the hair blond, the moonlight more romantic. This time the print was titled and copyrighted. It was called, simply, *Alone*. Perfect. And only twenty-five dollars. Later that afternoon, Heather didn't feel well, so she sat on a bench while I continued to wander. Ten minutes later I ran back to her, laughing, "You're not going to believe this! You have to come see this, I don't care how sick you are."

"Don't tell me you've found another one of those paintings," she guessed. But I wouldn't tell her, made her come see for herself. And there it was. This time the colors were vivid, almost lurid. The skirt was red, the moonlight Technicolor, the clouds dramatic. But the girl's head hung low, her braid flowed, and the sea died into the horizon. It was a print again, unfortunately set into a very expensive frame, which I didn't want. The owner thought I was odd when I asked if I could buy just the picture, but he sold it to me for ten dollars, even kindly spent a long time prying it from the frame.

All four versions now share the wall opposite my bed. I remember buying the first one, how fragile I was, how the image made me want to cry, how hesitant I was to talk to the antiques dealer for fear she would guess, or inadvertently say the wrong thing. Seeing them all grouped together makes me smile ruefully at how easily self-pity comes, and how pathetic it is. There is a time for sitting, slumped, with my head bowed, and there always will be, but there are also times that call for joy, for throwing my head back and laughing, in spite of everything. I have been forced by circumstance to retreat to my original plan, to lead an interesting life, and am determined to make the best of it.

Another birthday. I realize suddenly that somehow, without my noticing, time became almost normal again. Not the first year, but the next, or maybe the one after, the months picked up speed. At first, the bulk of the year was filler, to be endured until the next summer upstate. I was subconsciously breaking up the year into manageable parts. Work was nothing more than a paycheck, something to allow me to take time off, until, surreptitiously, it became interesting again, and, at times, fun. I try to observe life as a scenic artist, rather than as a widow. I capture scenes in mental snapshots, so that I can re-create them, to sharpen my memory. Paying attention is more rewarding than trying not to see; it is my nature.

There are still, even now, days without end, but they are mostly confined to empty weekends, the loneliest time, when there are too many couples and families out and about. I allow myself a periodic "wallow" day, but try not to let it endure beyond twenty-four hours, and recognize it for what it is, a momentary, if necessary, lapse. There are still nights that only Scotch and half an antihistamine will get me through, but they are further and further apart. I feel too horrible the next day, too old. I worry that as time passes I forget too much, how it felt to be loved and cherished. But then I think that maybe that is what makes life bearable—not to remember how it once was, how I thought it would be.

Sometimes I think that the aging process is nothing more than inuring myself to loss. Or maybe it's that none of the deaths, no matter how grievous, can rip the fabric of my life to shreds as Paul's did. It seems that there's not enough space to recover between funerals, but each time I pull myself together, choose something black from my closet, and clench my teeth through another ceremony. As those I love demonstrate each time a variation on dying, this one a slow fading, that one a hopeless, violent explosion, they add to a wellspring of sorrow which, paradoxically, forces me to treasure the appreciation I have found again for life. Complementary colors, those that are opposites, like purple and yellow, or red and green, when put side by side are more vibrant, more radiant. Death can have that effect on life. But complementary colors, when mixed together, turn muddy, unpleasant, and death can color life that way, as well. It is never so simple as one or the other, but is in constant flux, like a whirling kaleidoscope.

As I reached my fortieth birthday, I wondered where the years went, forgetting how long each minute once lasted. I am beginning to feel so much older than Paul, loving a man as I leave him behind in what seems like youth, forever thirty-three. Instead of a year younger than I, he is three years younger, then six years younger, and so on. As he recedes into the distance, time forces me into the present.

On my thirty-seventh birthday, I decided to climb a mountain, nothing too difficult. There was a story in one of my guidebooks that was appealing, about Mount Jo, a smallish mountain in the high-peaks region. In 1877, a wealthy man, Henry von Hoevenberg, hiked to the top of Mount Marcy, the highest peak in the Adirondacks, with his fiancée, and told her to choose from all the land, as far as she could see, the spot where she would like him to build the home they would live in after they married. She saw far beneath them a heart-shaped lake, and chose its shore. Her name was Josephine, hence "Mount Jo"; the lake is called Heart Lake. She died within the year, before the house was finished. It was eventually completed, only to be destroyed in a forest fire in 1903.

When I arrived, the sky was the color of wet cement; by the time I climbed halfway, it was raining lightly, the trail a ribbon of slippery mud, churned deeply in spots. Because it is an easy hike, because the fall foliage was at its dazzling peak, there were many people, mostly families, dozens with children. The crowds and the weather combined to make me miserable, and I wanted to be done with feeling miserable. I practically ran to the top, "Excuse me, excuse me," the whole way as I rushed past the dawdlers gawking at the view. I was determined to reach the top but had no wish to prolong the experience. I glanced summarily at the spectacular view, then quickly descended, yearning for the comfort of my solitude. By the time I arrived home, the clouds had relented, allowing the sun to feebly warm my birthday swim in Paradox Lake. I realized with chagrin that a new tradition had begun; not only did I have to swim each year on my birthday, now I have to climb a mountain as well. For my fortieth, I chose Ampersand, for good luck, although I was almost blown off the windswept summit, and then swam in both Lower Saranac and Paradox Lakes. I spent a glorious day alone.

The water temperature falls with the passing weeks. There is something unnatural in swimming when the leaves have turned, a sense that it is the wrong time to be going through this. But it adds a hint of something special to the ordeal. I can no longer swim in the morning or evening, but only at midday, needing every ounce of heat from the diminishing sun. There are carpenters building a house in the woods next to Lottie's. I don't like to be seen; I know they think I'm crazy. One day, when I'm pretending no one is over there, I notice one of them dip his hand in the water. "Man, this is freezing!" he exclaims. I am embarrassed.

I follow an established ritual. I arrive at the dock wearing my bathing suit, sweats, and flip-flops, the backpack over my shoulder holding my towel, bathing caps, goggles, anti-fog solution, earplugs, and eyeglass case—the essentials in life. I put the pack on a chair in the sun, spreading out the towel to absorb the warmth, so it will be there waiting for me. I take the temperature, mostly to reassure myself. I can make myself swim only because I know I have swum through much colder water. Sitting on the edge of the dock, I dangle my feet in the water in an attempt to see how closely I can predict what the thermometer will read.

The amount of time it takes to get into the water is inversely proportional to the temperature of the water. I stand, swinging my arms to loosen up. I spend quite a while stretching, trying to work up some heat, waiting, procrastinating. I remove my glasses, take the prescription goggles from their blue nylon bag, dribble anti-fog solution in them, then wipe them clean. I tuck up my hair, so much now that it barely fits, under two bathing caps, a fluorescent latex cap over a thick silicone one. I step out of my flip-flops, then my sweatpants. I put on my goggles so I am ready to go as soon as I can take off my sweatshirt, which is removed slowly, in stages, arms out of the sleeves but lingering inside the warmth, until I can bear to pull the fleecy cotton over my head.

Wet suits are forbidden under marathon-swimming rules, so I wear only a thin lycra Speedo. Still dry, already shivering, I cling to the top of the ladder, gingerly lowering one foot to the next rung, which is underwater. The scalding cold searing the sole of my foot is familiar, almost comforting. I know that I have been here before, and that in time it will not feel so bad. It is much easier at the end of the season, like coming back down a mountain. I know that when it hurts too much I can stop, and wait until it is time to start again in the spring. I can no longer swim in water as cold as during the summer of the English Channel. I have nothing to prove, I swim only for myself and am unwilling to put myself through that pain. But I am not content anymore with simply staring at the water from the shore. Once again, I find myself drawn to swimming, to immersion, to testing my limits.

The hair on my arms stands straight up, whitish-blond against my fading tan, the goose bumps almost comical. The muscles in my arms tense as I slowly, excruciatingly, lower one foot to the next rung, then the other foot. I gasp, smiling at my reluctance. Come on, you wimp, this is nothing, I chide myself. You've been in water this temperature for hours and hours. Why are you being such a baby? And I lower my foot one last time. The bottom rung is waist-deep, neck-deep when I scrunch down. Every spring I think about begging Lottie to add one more rung to the ladder, but by summer, when she is in Paradox, I have forgotten, and by autumn, when I remember, she is gone. I pant noisily as I inhale and exhale.

I count to three, then count to three again, and often, again. Intuitively, for no particular reason, at a certain instant I find the courage and push off, only to regret it. Putting my head under is the worst part; the pain of submersion forces me back to the ladder, where I wait, gasping and shaking, but calm, mustering the strength to let go. It is almost easy the second time. I know I don't want to give up, and I know I don't have to stay in for long. I swim shorter distances when the water is cold; it is what I allow myself. But sometimes, once I start making my way through the water, I feel as if I could go forever. The tingling, the breathlessness, the intensity of the sensation send me flying. I think, Okay, I'll just swim to the island, but by the time I get there I think, This is so great, I might as well swim across the lake and back. My turnover is rapid, the energy generated by movement not only warms me but speeds me, hydroplaning, over the water. At first I ride high in a futile attempt to stay above the water, until eventually I relax, settle into my element. The density of the icy liquid gives me that much more to push against, that much greater a surge ahead with each stroke, or so I imagine.

When the water drops below 65 degrees, I wear earplugs, which muffle the gurgling of splashes and the bubbling of expelled air, helping to lull me into this energetic state of grace. And I am reminded of why I do these things I do: to feel alive in every molecule of my body, to stay awake, to shock myself into motion. It is a mystery to me, as I return to the dock feeling undeniably wonderful, how I could have made it past the point when it hurt so cruelly, how I trusted I would benefit from the cold once past the initial pain.

I almost managed to swim through to Paul's birthday that first summer, lasting until the twenty-seventh. And then it flurried on the twenty-eighth—not enough to stick, but enough to make it seem too wintry to get back in the water. The snow blew in on a frigid, blustery wind. I visited the dock wearing a sweater and jeans and a jacket and a scarf and mittens, and knew I wouldn't be able to stand there clothed in any less. I am eager to return to the city, even though I will suffer through the winter swimming within the warm confines of an indoor pool, feeling like a shark in an aquarium made for guppies, waiting impatiently for spring, even as I dread walking into the water that first time. Most of my memories are of the wonders of open-water swimming, not the pain; the beauty, not the fears.

Five years after Paul's death I have swum into October; my earliest swim thus far was May 8. Five months isn't a bad outdoor season, especially for the Adirondacks. When I first found my house, I fretted that the closest indoor pool was so far away. That was before I fell in love with the long distances of open-water swimming. If I hadn't trained to swim the English Channel, I never would have known to what degree I could bear the cold.

I have a photograph that Paul's father took many years ago. He had waited on the shore while I swam and Paul paddled beside me. We crossed to the other side of Paradox Lake, then turned around, not wanting Paul's father to get bored, or lonely. I felt that I hadn't swum a real workout, so I tied the canoe to my ankle, to provide drag, to force me to put more exertion into what was otherwise an effortless journey. In the picture, taken as we approached land, Paul sits holding the oar, broad side in the air, like a banner. He is relaxed, grinning. I am visible as a small froth of white, from my kick and the splash of orange that is my cap. The shot was taken between strokes, so both my arms are in the water, one poised to ease its way through the air, the other finishing its glide, already starting to pull back. The canoe would have been heavy on land, to say nothing of Paul's added weight, but once I was in motion, it had a momentum of its own. The rope around my ankle bit in as it pulled taut, and chafed every so often as it took a wave differently than I did, but mostly it floated easily behind me, always there, never to be forgotten.